# What People are Saying About
## *The Trust Edge*

"Trust is the most important fundamental between leaders and among people. It is the cornerstone for building lasting relationships and growing successful business enterprises. This book shows you exactly how to build the 8 Pillars of Trust and how to apply them for maximum effectiveness."—*Dr. Nido Qubein, Chairman, Great Harvest Bread Co. and President, High Point University*

"Gripping and insightful! Anyone wanting to take his or her leadership to the next level must read this book! It will become THE AUTHORITATIVE GUIDE on building Trust!"—*Alex Lopes, CEO, Progora*

"Horsager hits the mark in delivering his important message about the critical nature of trust in all relationships—whether between family, friends, business associates, or governments. Especially in these uncertain times we live in, David's insights should be embraced by everyone."—*Jim Hamilton, Director, National League of Cities, Risk Information Sharing Consortium*

"A breach of confidence in the aviation industry can have a catastrophic outcome. Horsager's book provides practical application of critical trust principles in a manner that will enhance the business relationships and bottom line in any industry."—*Steve Wareham, Airport Director, Minneapolis-St. Paul International Airport*

"This book is great for the soul—not to mention business. Horsager's 8 Pillars of Trust supply the nourishment we need to be successful in life and business. It's a book to read and reread to keep us fortified."
—*Carol Odell, CEO, Better Business Bureau–Southern Colorado*

"David is right on the money. Trust is the lubricant of high-performing working relationships. *The Trust Edge* provides a comprehensive behavioral blueprint to integrate the 8 essential Pillars of Trust into your organization. This is a must read book for organizational leaders and their supervisors."—*Larry Cole, Ph.D., CEO, TeamMax®, and author of* People-$mart Leaders

"David Horsager's book, *The Trust Edge*, is a powerful resource for leaders. As I read it, I kept thinking: *We need to do this! This would make us more effective!* This well-written, well-conceived, well-documented book demonstrates the importance of trust. Horsager's practical tips and illustrations will help any organization increase its effectiveness if it is willing to build on the foundational pillars he describes. *The Trust Edge* will pay dividends for smart companies!"
—*Jay Barnes, President, Bethel University*

"I wholeheartedly support the lessons that David outlines in *The Trust Edge*. I am a big believer in authenticity. The more people get to know and see the real person, the more likely they are to extend their trust."—*Mike Tattersfield, President and CEO, Caribou Coffee Company*

"I found *The Trust Edge* to be tangible, extremely practical, and relevant. I will personally hand this out to every leader in my organization."
—*Mike Cylkowski, Operating Partner, Keller Williams Integrity*

"*The Trust Edge* has valuable lessons, not only for business professionals, but also for individuals looking for guidance in their own personal development. Trust—that's what it's all about!"—*Larry N. Swenson, President, Noel International*

"David Horsager gets it right when he says, 'Trust is not a soft skill. It is a measurable competency that affects outcomes more than anything else.' You simply cannot put a price on the kind of trust Horsager talks about. Trust is our competitive advantage."—*Anthony Diekemper, CEO, Earth Security Electronics*

"At a time when our confidence in political, economical, and social institutions is at its lowest level in recent history, David Horsager shows us the path to rebuilding both trust and success."—*Matt Kinne, Administrator Walker Methodist Health Center*

"Riveting and Insightful! Horsager concisely reveals *The Trust Edge* roadmap that will take you and your team to a whole new level! Jam-packed with hard-hitting, real-world examples, this book is a MUST READ for anyone who wants to grow as a leader! You really owe it to your team to buy and read this book!"—*Ed Clark, President and CEO, ServiceMaster Clean, Midwest Region*

"*The Trust Edge* is full of insight into not only why the right things remain fundamental, but also how to go about them in daily life and in business. Trust must be earned and habits must be formed. Anyone with an interest in improving their personal relationships will not be able to put this book down. They will also find an amazingly quick impact in their business life. They will be changed and people will notice."—*Steven Grandchamp, President and CEO, OpenLogic*

"*The Trust Edge* is not a quick fix, but an investment—a legacy of wisdom. It should be leather-bound for life's journey. David has tapped into a rich reservoir of personal experiences as a master educator, parent, and husband."—*Jeff Edson, CFO, Lyle Signs*

"David has nailed the trust issue. His book shines a bright light on the impact trust has on every aspect of our lives. We can all gain valuable insight from *The Trust Edge*."—*Bill Schult, CEO, Maximum Potential*

"Based on research but written for practical use by real-life leaders, *The Trust Edge* takes a fresh look at the foundation of genuine success—TRUST. At Kemps, we believe that building trust creates a sustainable competitive advantage."—*Jim Green, President and CEO, Kemps*

"David Horsager shows you the process to develop and build trust in any situation. If you don't have trust, you have nothing. In spite of what some people say, making your way in the world is all about trust."—*Thomas J. Winninger, Chairman, Winninger Companies and Ascendancy Research*

"*The Trust Edge* clearly lays out the 8 Pillars of Trust that are foundational for the starting point of all working relationships."—*Dr. Dennis S. Reina, Ph.D., Co-Author, Trust & Betrayal in the Workplace: Building Effective Relationships in Your Organization*

"David Horsager takes a broad look at trust as a business success measure and offers practical suggestions that will resonate with people across all industries."—*Philomena Morrissey Satre, VP Diversity & Inclusion, Wells Fargo*

"When we are intentional about striving to conduct ourselves in a manner that makes us worthy of trust, the natural by-product is that people will want to associate with us and do business with us. David Horsager's book will give you the tools needed to live such a life."
—*Bill Forbes, General Manager, A1 Automotive Services*

"Any enterprise seeking to improve its financial and operational performance will benefit from the principles in Horsager's work on trust. *The Trust Edge* is a principle-centered yet practical approach to sustained individual and organizational success."—*Ken Morris, JD, former VP, Boston Scientific, current President, Apercu Group*

"David Horsager is on target—leadership begins from within and fundamentally depends on trust. If you aspire to leadership, park your ego at the door, cultivate a quiet mind, and study the road ahead. Trust and humility are fundamental."—*Dr. Massoud Amin, Distinguished Professor and Director, Technological Leadership Institute, University of Minnesota*

"WOW, *The Trust Edge* is based on the #1 principle that I use when I go in to turn around a company! There is nothing more important than TRUST. When established in the proper framework, it becomes the path for increased profits, productivity, morale, output, and most importantly, customer and employee retention. I love the book. You have placed in print the very essence of my leadership success—THANK YOU!"—*Ronald E. Lentz, CEO, WLG, USA group, and CEO, World Commerce Services*

# THE
# TRUST
# EDGE

*How Top Leaders Gain Faster*
*Results, Deeper Relationships,*
*and a Stronger Bottom Line*

## DAVID HORSAGER

summerside
*PRESS™*

Summerside Press™
Minneapolis 55438
www.summersidepress.com
*The Trust Edge*
© 2009, 2010 by David Horsager

ISBN 978-1-60936-133-4

Unattributed quotations are by David Horsager.

Published in association with the literary agency of WordServe
Literary Group, Ltd., www.wordservliterary.com

Cover and interior design by Purpose Design

Author photos © 2010 by David Horsager

*Summerside Press™ is an inspirational publisher offering fresh,
irresistible books to uplift the heart and engage the mind.*


For bulk discounts
or other *Trust Edge* resources,
call 1-800-608-8969
email info@TheTrustEdge.com
or visit www.TheTrustEdge.com

## Dedication

*To my wife*, Lisa, my most trusted partner.

*To my parents*, Clarence and Mary,
who taught me more about trust than
any amount of research ever would.

*To my four precious children*,
Vanessa, Isaiah, Maria Claire, and Micah.
One of my greatest hopes is that you will earn
and enjoy *The Trust Edge*.

*To God*, who is worthy of my trust.

# Contents

# Acknowledgments

M any people have given me a glimpse into what trust in leadership really means. My parents trusted me with heavy farm machinery at a very young age. A farm is a great place to learn about trust. Being trusted by Minnesota's most winning high school football coach helped me become an All-State player. I was entrusted with an organization early in my career when I could have been seen as too young and inexperienced to handle the job.

My in-laws trusted me with their daughter. And most importantly, my wife, Lisa, trusted me enough to say, "Yes!" She is my trusted partner. I am so thankful for her unwavering support and encouragement, and also for her genuine trust in God. Without her this project would not have happened. I am most grateful to God for His many blessings, and I strive to be faithful with all that He has entrusted to me.

As with everything I have done of any value in life, many talented and willing people have been involved. It is the same in this project. I thank my close friends and advisors, Joe Kimbell, Scott Lundeen, and Jason Sheard, my incredible editor and friend, Heidi Sheard. Thanks to my fantastic designer and friend, Heidi Koopman, who always delivers more than expected. She captured my vision for the design of this book and took it to another level. Thanks to friends Connie

Anderson, Patricia Angulo, Christopher Batdorf, Ross Bernstein, Dr. Jolene K. Beuhrer, Tim and Brenda Cimbura, Meghan Donner, Clarice Esslinger, Sam Helgerson, Loren Horsager, Kent and Beth Horsager, Dr. Ron Hultgren, Brandon Johnson, Lori La Bey, Alex Lopes, Spencer Moffatt, Tom O'Lenick, Nate Parks, John and Sue Parks, Kris Rydberg, and Jonathon Stuart, all gave input and insights into this project. Thanks to the Boys Doing Business group and my Horsager Leadership team. Thank you to my mentors and to the many organizations and audiences who have invited me to speak and consult—and in so doing helped me better understand the bottom-line impact of trust. Thank you to my alma mater, Bethel University, where my research for this project began.

Trust, not money, is the currency of business and life.

"Trust is the single largest driver of public attitude on a whole range of issues from globalization to terrorism to the role of governments. Trust also is the prime driver of corporate and country brands. As goes trust, so goes the world."[1]

—Doug Miller, President of GlobeScan

# Introduction

## 1111

"Mergers, downsizing, and globalization have accelerated the pace of change in organizations, creating a crisis of trust that didn't exist a generation ago."[2] —Robert F. Hurley, Fordham University

We are in a crisis. And our biggest crisis is not the financial one. This year at the World Economic Forum in China, world leaders got it right when they declared that our *biggest* crisis is a lack of trust and confidence. We are in a *trust crisis* and organizations are slow to realize the bottom-line implications.

Trust has always been foundational to genuine success of any kind. However, it has not been labeled as such. People seldom talk about trust as a competency to learn and practice. That is changing. Almost overnight, trust found its way into the public limelight specifically because it has been so hard to find. From massive fraud in business to scandals in politics and athletics, the headlines point to a persistent problem of modern life and business—we're lacking in trust. Meanwhile, the world is "flattening" in many respects. Cultures are meeting and expanding in ways that weren't possible even a decade ago. But globalization isn't a free ride. Joining the mega-mergers and open markets are new suspicions and misunderstandings. We can reach across borders, but we don't know how to be trusted by the people we find on the other side. In the 21st century, trust has become the world's most precious resource.

Trust has the ability to accelerate or destroy any business, organization, or relationship. The lower the trust, the more time everything takes, the more everything costs, and the lower the loyalty of everyone involved. However, greater trust brings superior innovation, creativity, freedom, morale, and productivity.

---

Trust is a requirement for strong friendships, families, and firms.

---

Before I started my graduate research based on trust, I had been searching for the uniqueness of top leaders and organizations. Top leaders were defined as ones who were not only successful financially, but also made a significant positive influence in the lives of those they served over a period of time. Top leaders left individuals and organizations measurably better than they found them. What made these people and organizations unique? They all had one common trait—trust. I found that trust is not a soft skill. It is a measurable competency that brings dramatic results. It can be built into an organization's strategy, goals, and culture.

My experience, fueled by this fresh research, led me to a fascination with the bottom-line impact of trust. I began a journey to research the commonalities of the most trusted leaders and organizations. The journey has resulted in this book, based in research, but made very practical with stories, anecdotes, and simple practical steps to help you gain *The Trust Edge*.

Read each chapter and think about how you can apply it. Take time to reflect and review. There are questions at the end of the chapters to help you cement ideas and use them in your situation. Better yet, meet in a group to brainstorm and act on the best takeaways. My hope is that you will be inspired to implement these strategies and thereby enjoy the great benefits of *The Trust Edge* in your life and organization.

## The Pillars

If you visit the Roman ruins or the synagogue in Capernaum, you will see that many parts of the structures have crumbled, but the pillars still stand. The pillars are the foundation for holding something up. They are strong, solid, and lasting. In the years I've spent studying the underlying connection between success and trust, I've identified eight key areas that are best described as Pillars. They are the bedrock that creates *The Trust Edge*. These pillars are applicable for anyone interested in establishing a foundation for genuine success.

## Trust Impacts You

No matter your role, trust affects your influence and success. It impacts every level of business, from Fortune 500 leaders to a family-owned general store. It affects teaching outcomes and political votes. Those who are trusted are effective.

"Without trust, influence diminishes."[3]

—Vanessa Hall, Australian management expert and author

**Impact of having *The Trust Edge*:**

- Leaders will see expanded influence and increased morale.
- Managers will see greater productivity and increased commitment from teams.
- Sales people will see increased engagement and results.
- Service experts will see enthusiastic recommendations and loyal customers.
- Parents will see more peace and freedom at home.
- Teachers will see more respect, impact, and classroom control.

## The Main Point

Though we will discuss trusting others later in the book, helping individuals and organizations become trusted is the main point. Resist the urge to think about others and whether or not they deserve to be trusted. Take responsibility for *yourself.* When you focus on increasing *your Trust Edge*, you will enjoy greater success and impact. When you change yourself, you have the best chance of impacting your organization, family, relationships, and even your world.

⌒||||⌒

**Note on subject and sourcing:** After years of research and study, trust and its impact has become a passion of mine. While I hope to have brought fresh insight and practicality to an old subject, I understand that thoughts and ideas from a variety of sources have been running in my mind for years. While I have sought to diligently source this book project, please know any failure to give full and proper credit is purely unintentional.

# PART I

## THE CASE
## FOR TRUST

Everything of value
is built on trust,
from financial systems
to relationships.

*Chapter One*

# The Trust Edge

## ⌢1111⌣

---

"To be trusted is a greater compliment than being loved."

—George MacDonald, Scottish Author, Poet, and Theologian

---

When I come home from work, my kids often greet me at the door. It is my 3-year-old son who runs up to me and pulls on my pant leg. He has excited eyes and a great big smile. He shouts, "Daddy, Daddy, throw me up in the air really HIGH." He loves to get tossed up in the air. "Daddy, throw me up in the air really HIGH!" And so I do.

And, most of the time...I catch him.

No. He trusts his daddy to catch him every single time—and I do! This is trust in its purest form.

It is similar to the transactions of business and life. Without trust, the transactions cannot occur. Without trust, influence is destroyed. Without trust, leaders lose teams. Without trust, people lose sales. Without trust, organizations lose productivity, relationships, reputation, talent retention, customer loyalty, creativity, morale, revenue, and results. They lose in their brand and in their bottom line. John O. Whitney, Director of the Deming Center for Quality Management at the Columbia Business School found, "Mistrust doubles the cost of doing business."[1]

In one of the largest and most extensive surveys of its kind, Watson Wyatt studied 12,750 U.S. workers in all major industries and work levels. According to the study, "Companies with high trust levels generated total returns to shareholders at almost three times that of companies with low levels of trust."[2] Whether you are a student or a CEO, a teacher or a parent, a politician or a nurse, trust multiplies influence and impact. Before we get too far, let's define *The Trust Edge*.

---

"In my business, there is nothing more important than trust."[3]

—Harvey Mackay, CEO, Mackay Envelope Company

---

## Trust Defined

Trust is a confident belief in someone or something. It is the confident belief in an entity:

- To do what is right,
- To deliver what is promised,
- To be the same every time, in spite of the circumstances.

Trust speaks to being reliable, dependable, and capable. Think of the chair you are sitting on as an example. You have a confident belief that it can and will hold you. You don't need to waste time checking its capacity. You don't worry about it taking advantage of you or dropping you. The trust your chair has earned has affected the speed, consistency, and loyalty of you doing "business" with it.

You are trusted to the degree that people believe in your ability, your consistency, your integrity, and your commitment to deliver. Do people believe in you? To the degree that they do, you are trusted.

---

Trust: A confident belief in a person, product, or organization.

---

## Why the "Edge"

When I was studying top organizations and leaders, I found that some clearly had a competitive edge over others. Those leaders or organizations that could weather storms, charge higher prices, maintain respect with customers and clients, and foster long-term growth were special. The greatest leaders and organizations of all time have had the same competitive edge. They were the most trusted. Robert F. Hurley, the Founding Director of the Fordham Center for Entrepreneurship, was right when he wrote, "Leaders who understand how trust is built can actively influence its development, resulting in a more supportive and productive work environment and, not incidentally, a competitive advantage."[4] *The Trust Edge* is the competitive advantage gained when others confidently believe in you!

## Like a Forest

Have you seen the magnificent forest at Redwood National Park in Northern California? The oldest recorded Redwood is over 2,200 years old! Redwoods can be well over a football field length high and more than 20 feet in diameter.[5] A lush and beautiful Redwood forest takes many years to deepen roots, grow branches, and flourish. And yet one poor decision with one small match can take it all down in a fraction of the time it took to mature. Trust is like that. While it may appear to be static, in reality trust is more like a forest—a long time growing, but easily burned down with a touch of carelessness. Trust requires time, effort, diligence, and character. Inspiring trust is not slick or easy to fake. If you were looking for instant gratification or a quick fix, you might be disappointed by the truths of this book. If however, you are interested in following the only way to genuine, lasting success in relationships, work, or life, this book is for you! *The Trust Edge*. Build it, protect it, and ultimately enjoy the benefits of a strong trust forest with rooted relationships and high-yield results.

---

"It took an average of seven months for employees to build their trust in a leader but less than half that time for them to lose it."[6] —Manchester Consulting

---

## Dimensions of Trust

There are two dimensions of trust. First, there is the dimension of time. This dimension goes from short to long. As I mentioned in the forest analogy, it generally takes a long time to grow; yet it can be lost in a short time. Another aspect of time is that most trust starts to be established very quickly. It is almost a gut feeling. Most people can talk to someone for two minutes and decide if they are going to start to trust them or not.

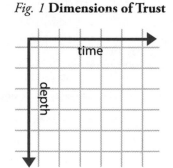

*Fig. 1* **Dimensions of Trust**

Another dimension of trust is depth. This dimension goes from shallow to deep. Deep trust is generally established over time. It can withstand adversity and is often born of personal experiences. Deep trust often sprouts up quickly if a trusted source testifies that you are trustworthy. I call this Transferred Trust. Because A trusts B, and B trusts C, then A trusts C. Transferred Trust can happen with less effort on your part, but it still depends on the depth of trust gained with the first person.

*Fig. 2* **Transferred Trust**

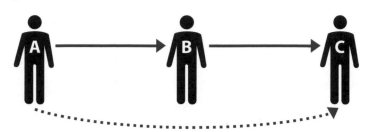

Time and depth interact in several ways. While it might be lost in a moment, once trust is deeply rooted and strong, it can often withstand many storms and challenges. These thoughts are not contradictory, but rather just proof of the great scope of this concept we call trust. When trust is deeply established, you will often be given the benefit of the doubt instead of having every action judged with skepticism. So the dimensions of trust, "depth" and "time," are in constant interplay and have a huge influence on the strength of your trustworthiness.

A musical score provides an analogy to simplify this concept. Have you ever listened to an orchestra and found yourself moved by the power of the music? Bach, Beethoven, and other famous composers are masters at combining notes with the dimensions of time and depth to create

PART I

CLARITY

COMPASSION

CHARACTER

COMPETENCY

COMMITMENT

CONNECTION

CONTRIBUTION

CONSISTENCY

PART III

PART IV

PART V

powerful music. Types of trust, when influenced by the right dimensions of time and depth, can also produce powerful results.

Although there are two dimensions and several types of trust, there is only one way to earn it! Establish it by personally building the **Eight Pillars of Trust** discussed in this book. When they are part of your character, your trustworthiness exudes from you in all interactions.

## Not Just a "Soft Skill"

Trust is tangible, learnable, and measurable. Trust is not simply a dish on your leadership buffet. It is the table holding up the smorgasbord of talent demonstrated by your team every day. The exciting part is when your buffet table increases, others both inside and outside of your organization will begin bringing their skills and abilities to add to the table. It is surprising to me that so many managers search for so-called "hard" skills instead of looking for the most important skills. For example, sales people get caught up in seeking the newest sales tip or closing technique, but without trust, they won't even get in the door. With trust there is no need for the newest tactic. When organizations acquire *The Trust Edge*, it shows in every relationship and eventually is proved by a growing bottom line. Trust gives a concrete and critical advantage.

---

Companies with high trust levels outperform companies with low trust levels by 186%.[7] —Watson Wyatt, WorkUSA®

---

# The Trust Edge

¶ In the 21st century, trust has become the world's most precious resource.

¶ Costs are high when trust is low.

¶ Trust is a confident belief in a person, product, or organization.

¶ While it may appear to be static, trust is more like a forest—a long time growing, but easily burned down with a touch of carelessness.

¶ Being talented is valuable, but being trusted is the fundamental key to anyone's genuine success.

## Ask Yourself ...

1. How does trust impact you or your role?

   _____

   _____

   _____

2. How would you define *The Trust Edge*?

   _____

   _____

   _____

3. What are the dimensions of trust?

   _____

   _____

4. How do the dimensions influence one another?

   _____

   _____

5. Whom do you trust? Why?

   _____

   _____

   _____

   _____

Trust multiplies
influence
and impact.

A lack of trust
is your biggest
expense.

*Chapter Two*

# Impact of Trust

⌒
]]]]
⌒

---

"Trust reduces transaction costs; it reduces the need for litigation and speeds commerce; it actually lubricates organizations and societies."[1]
—Marilyn Carlson Nelson, Chairman and CEO, Carlson Companies

---

## Against the Odds

In 2009, amidst one of the worst economies in America, a small privately owned software development company, Passlogix, won prepaid contracts worth millions of dollars in an industry where that is not the norm. Incredibly, they beat out established software giants such as IBM to earn the business. Why is Passlogix thriving? Trust. Why will clients pay in advance? Trust. According to author and analyst Peter Bregman, Passlogix has trust that others do not for several reasons.

1. They have built the business on personal relationships. If any work is not done to expectations, clients know they can call CEO Marc Boroditsky themselves.

2. Boroditsky frequently tells clients and colleagues of his personal commitment to them. In turn his employees share it with customers, and there has become a culture of commitment and confidence.

3. While a large company gave a sense of security in the past, a smaller more agile and accountable company gains trust today. The big players need bailouts, but the smaller ones tend to take full responsibility and enjoy the benefits of trusted client relationships.[2]

## Trust Affects the Bottom Line

You might have heard this great story before, but Jason Kottke's experience in New York City is a straightforward account about the impact of trust.

> *"Next!" said the coffee & doughnut man (whom I'll refer to as "Ralph") from his tiny silver shop-on-wheels, one of many that dot Manhattan on weekday mornings. I stepped up to the window, ordered a glazed doughnut (75 cents), and when he handed it to me, I tried to hand a dollar bill back through the window. Ralph motioned me toward the pile of change scattered on the counter and hurried on to the next customer, yelling "Next!" over my shoulder. I put the bill down and grabbed a quarter from the pile.*
>
> *Maybe this situation is typical of Manhattan coffee and doughnut carts (although two carts near where I work don't do this), but this was the first business establishment I've ever been to that lets its customers make their own change. Intrigued, I walked a few steps away and turned around to watch the interaction between this business and its customers. For five minutes, everyone either threw down exact change or made*

*their own change without any notice from Ralph; he was just too busy pouring coffee or retrieving crullers to pay any attention to the money situation.*

*If you were the CEO of a big business—say, a movie studio, music company, or multinational bank—you'd have been tearing your hair out at this scene. He lets his customers make their own change! How does he know they're making the correct change? Or putting down any change at all? Or even stealing the change? Where's the technology that prevents the change from being stolen while he's not looking?*

*Ralph probably does lose a little bit of change each day to theft and bad math, but more than makes up for it in other ways. The throughput of that tiny stand is amazing. For comparison's sake, I staked out two nearby doughnut & coffee stands and their time spent per customer was almost double that of Ralph's stand. So, Ralph does roughly twice the business with the same resources.*

*It's also apparent that Ralph trusts his customers, and that they both appreciate and return that sense of trust (I know I do). Trust is one of the most difficult "assets" for companies to acquire, but also one of the most valuable. Many companies take shortcuts in getting their customers to trust them, paying lip service to trust in press releases and marketing brochures. Which works, temporarily and superficially, but when you get down to it, you can't market trust...it needs to be earned. People trust you when you [do the right things].*

*When an environment of trust is created, good things start happening. Ralph can serve twice as many customers. People get their coffee in half the time. Due to this time savings, people become regulars. Regulars provide Ralph's business with stability, a good reputation, and with customers who have an interest in making correct change (to keep the line moving and keep Ralph in business). Lots of customers who make correct change increase Ralph's profit margin.[3]*

Research agrees with Ralph. Trust, not money, is the currency of business and life. In a climate of trust, people are more creative, motivated, productive, and willing to sacrifice for the team. What happens when a business gains *The Trust Edge*? Every aspect of business becomes more profitable. Customers will pay more, tell others, and come back. With suppliers whom you trust, one call is enough. Delivery time and costs decrease because of less double checking, paperwork, and follow-up.

*Fig. 1* **As Trust Increases**

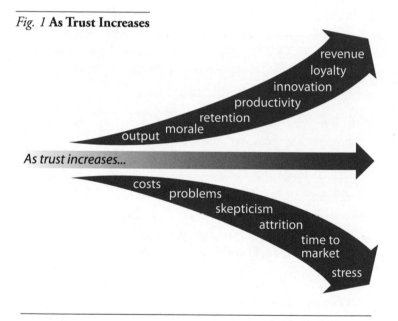

The link between employees' trust in leadership and firm performance is quite clear; as trust increases, firm performance rises.[4]

—SAM Advanced Management Journal, 2008

# The High Cost of Suspicion

Skepticism and suspicion create the opposite of trust and destroy motivation, teamwork, and results. Skepticism brings everything into question, slows processes, and promotes suspicion. America's trust climate has been rocked by suspicion. For just a glimpse of how this has happened, consider insurance scandals, New York and Illinois Governor misconduct, mortgage and banking meltdown, financial fraud and Ponzi schemes, Big Three Automakers' failings, executive greed that has bilked investors and employees, food contaminations, and athletes hiding drug use. It is no wonder suspicion is soaring. There is a cost.

> "Eighty percent of people stop buying products or services from companies when their trustworthiness comes into question."[5]
> —Edelman 2005 Trust Barometer

In fact, research from a study of 453 buyer-supplier relationships of automakers dealing in three countries (Japan, South Korea, and the United States), gave empirical evidence of the economic value of trust. The research found that the automakers' transaction costs were five times higher with the least trusted supplier than with the most trusted supplier. Further, with the least trusted suppliers, face-to-face interaction time doubled. Low trust revealed a need to spend more time and resources for communication, negotiation, and compliance. High trust led to greater information sharing and a willingness to sacrifice for the partner.[6]

> "The level of trust in business relationships...is a greater determinant of success than anything else, including content excellence."[7]
> —Charles H. Green, executive educator and author

**A lack of trust is your biggest expense.** As trust goes down, procedures and laws also increase, even on those who can be trusted. As a result, millions of dollars that could be used for research, staff training, or benefits and incentives, are being spent on oversight and accountability processes to accommodate regulations. Take the Patriot Act or Sarbanes-Oxley Act (SOA). The intent of both was to increase trust. However, the cost of either on business has been enormous. For instance, the first year SOA compliance costs for the average company were projected at $2 million. For a large company, one with more than $5 billion in revenue, the costs of first-year compliance topped $4.6 million. It does not take long to see the high cost of suspicion.[8]

---

"Trust forms the foundation for effective communication, associate retention, motivation, and contributions of discretionary energy."[9]

—Susan M. Heathfield, human resource expert and author

---

When people trust a company:

- 91% chose to buy from them
- 76% recommend them to a friend
- 55% will pay a premium to do business with them
- 42% share positive experiences online
- 26% bought shares

When people distrust a company:

- 77% refused to buy from them
- 72% criticized them to a friend or colleague
- 34% shared negative company experiences online
- 17% sold shares[10]

—Edelman 2009 Trust Barometer

"Without trust, there's no way that any organization can sustain innovation. Because without trust, no one is willing to take the risks that innovation requires."[11] —Dennis Stauffer, Founder of Insight Fusion Inc. and thought leader on innovation

## Trust Score

Your credit score is really a trust score. If a bank trusts you based on past financial responsibility, then you will get a higher score and pay less for a loan. In fact, I just asked my mortgage broker what the cost of a loan is today using different credit (trust) scores. She said if you have a score of 720, which is not a terribly high score, you can get a 30-year mortgage at 4.75 percent. However, if your credit score is 640, which is not a terribly low score, the best loan you can get would be at 7.25 percent. That means the less-trusted buyer will pay over $115,000 more on the same $200,000 mortgage. If you were to buy a half-million dollar house and had the lower credit score you would pay nearly $300,000 more over the course of the loan—and that does not account for the higher payments for insurance because of the lower credit score. The more you are trusted, the less you pay![12]

## Trustonomics

The impact of trust on the economy can be witnessed at the corporate level. Bear Stearns, AIG, and Lehman Brothers were at one time considered trust-based businesses. Each of these companies relied on the trust of the market to establish the firm's value. As trust goes down, value goes down. For instance, the $236 million purchase proposal for Bear Stearns by JP Morgan Chase came just hours after Bear Stearns' market capitalization was $3 billion. Interestingly, just over a year ago that market cap was $20 billion. As trust in the market tanks, so does the value of the business.[13]

Bill Otis, former Chief of the Appellate Division in the U.S. Attorney's Office, offered this analysis: "Our ability to bail our way out of this recession is extremely limited, because, even if they worked and could be paid for, bailouts and government spending generally fail to address the fundamental problem at the heart of our difficulties. The fundamental problem is not liquidity or even solvency. It is trust—or more correctly, the lack of trust—that has spawned the breakdown in the credit markets. The lack of trust cannot be remedied with money. It can only be remedied with that which creates trust."[14]

---

"We need to move extremely fast in restoring public confidence."[15] —Christine Lagarde, Minister of Economy, Industry and Employment of France

---

Though our trust has been shaken in America during this economic crisis, we still enjoy a level of trust that is not enjoyed in all parts of the world. A business professor and friend of mine, Leo Gabriel, was asked by a native of a small war-torn, developing country, "Why does capitalism work in America and not here?" Gabriel said, "Because, generally, we can assume trust in our economic system." In America we can go online, order a product, and assume it will be shipped. The retailer can generally assume that he will be paid. Without trust there cannot be economic activity. You must be able to put trust in your cash, check, or credit to have value and be good. A retailer must know that the product or service will be delivered from the supplier as expected. With greater trust comes greater economic activity and a better form of capitalism.

"Trust is key to restoring investor confidence. Rebuilding trust
requires business to think and communicate differently."[16]
—Richard Edelman, CEO, Edelman (world's largest public relations firm)

## Radio Returns

Most podcasts or blogs never lead to any more than a little extra
pocket cash. One podcaster has beaten the odds with a most unusual
approach. Canadian Stefan Molyneux is the innovative host of
Freedomain Radio, the largest philosophy podcast on the Internet
with over 4,000,000 Internet views per year. Molyneux has released
over 1,200 podcasts and at least seven books completely free of
charge. How does such a model produce any profit?

Freedomain Radio thrives on the honor system. Molyneux, in a
massive version of the office snack box, asks listeners to voluntarily
donate what value they find in the podcasts. He suggests $0.50 per
podcast. Molyneux believes Freedomain Radio's honor system has
resulted in a positive factor for his business model, which he didn't
entirely predict. The fact that his income could dry up at any minute
means that he feels a constant pull to keep producing relevant and
interesting podcasts. If he doesn't produce quality, people don't pay.
In my discussion with him he told me, "I get instant feedback. I
know right away if it was good or not based on how many donations
come in for that material."

Molyneux says he keeps the donation model so listeners feel ownership of the podcasts. Listeners engage and feel that they are a real part
of the conversation since they contribute to its financial success. His
sites include no advertising, and people don't even get to write-off
their donations because he is not a charity.

Molyneux proves that where there is trust, money will follow. "Trust is everything," Molyneux told me. "If I didn't have trust there would be no downloads, no show, and no business." According to him, the most important factor for trust is humility. Being humble has made him one of the most trusted philosophers of our time, because he is open to differing opinions and willing to bow to the good points and logic of others.

Another important aspect of trust is being congruent. Molyneux mentioned, "Your business model needs to be aligned with your content and your approach." Since his philosophy is that "people are basically good" and that "voluntary virtue is the best ideology," his donation model is consistent with his philosophy and business.

Stefan Molyneux has defined trust as the *best conceivable* principle to have in the modern marketplace, and it has resulted in success for his business.[17]

## Southwest Stays above the Clouds

As one of America's most beloved companies, Southwest Airlines (SWA) has posted consistent profits an amazing 35 years in a row in an industry where fuel costs, security concerns, and customer dissatisfaction have forced major competitors into bankruptcy.

While the airline industry, as a whole, has found itself rated below the IRS in customer satisfaction, SWA has consistently been ranked among the leaders, in any industry, in customer satisfaction, employee satisfaction, and corporate reputation.[18] SWA has been #1 in on-time arrivals, departures, and overall quality. It has been named "friendliest," "most reliable," and has won recognition for being one of the best places to work.[19] They also earned the top score in the University of Michigan's American Customer Satisfaction Index among U.S. carriers for the 16th straight year. They use only one kind of plane, Boeing 737s, to keep costs down. SWA has the youngest fleet of planes and incurs the lowest cost per available seat. A primary reason for their enduring success has been the trust they've established with their employees and their customers.[20]

In the spring of 2008 it came out that SWA missed several mandatory maintenance checks, operating dozens of their planes in violation of several federal laws. Facing a major fine by the FAA, the company's response was to ground the aircraft and release the personnel they deemed responsible. For most corporations, and especially an airline, this would spell a public relations nightmare! The outcry that would arise from the mere suggestion that lives were put at risk to secure a larger profit might be extreme. But for the most part, passengers failed to react at all. Why would they give Southwest a pass on what seems to be an egregious error? The public offered them an extra amount of grace because of the exceptional level of trust Southwest had achieved.

A couple of weeks after the story broke, a major news outlet sent a reporter on a Southwest flight to see how people were reacting to the story. One passenger seemed to capture the consensus: "They truly seem to care about their customers."[21] The customer's comments fall in line with this conclusion. Trust was restored.

If you happen to make a mistake that could erode trust, sometimes stakeholders will see your mistake as an exception and continue to have complete confidence in you. You can't count on it, but an extra measure of grace is commonly given to those who have shown pure intentions and a solid foundation of trust. On the rare occasion that a mistake is made, those who have *The Trust Edge* are given the benefit of the doubt.

As an entrepreneur, consultant, and speaker, I have often seen organizations put their focus on the trivial over the fundamental. In spite of the importance of trust in our business world today, few leaders have given it the focus it deserves. Trust is not a technique, like a negotiating tactic. It's the cornerstone that allows the negotiation to happen in the first place. The good news is that *The Trust Edge* is built on habits that can be formed. It can be fortified in an organization by implementing trusted systems.

## Beyond the Bottom Line

If the Pillars of Trust outlined in this book are practiced genuinely, I guarantee bottom-line results. One benefit of sincerely building trust is the priceless feeling that comes when one does what he knows in his heart is the right thing to do. Other intangibles of genuine trust include decreased stress and increased peace, fulfillment, solid friendships, and a lasting legacy.

The biggest deceiver is the one who appears trustworthy when in fact he is not. Because someone could learn to build the Pillars of Trust to manipulate them insincerely, should they not be taught? Of course they should. We teach our kids to say "thank you" and "please," hoping some day those words will come out of a thankful and kind heart, though we know kids simply do it at first because we ask them to. Even if you start building the Pillars because you "are asked to," my hope is that this foundation of trust will become a part of who you are. Then by earning *The Trust Edge*, you will gain a significant advantage that extends far beyond the bottom line.

PART I

CLARITY

COMPASSION

CHARACTER

COMPETENCY

COMMITMENT

CONNECTION

CONTRIBUTION

CONSISTENCY

PART III

PART IV

PART V

# The Impact of Trust

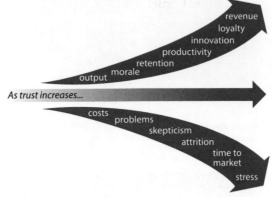

℡ Trust, not money, is the currency of business and life.

℡ For the trusted brand, people will pay more, come back, and tell others.

℡ A lack of trust is your biggest expense.

℡ Trust is a necessity for economic activity.

℡ The biggest deceiver is the one who appears trustworthy when in fact he is not.

℡ Trust is not a "soft" skill.

## Ask Yourself ...

1. How much does lack of trust cost your organization? Consider relationships, loyalty, retention, and influence.

   _____

   _____

   _____

2. What are the benefits of high trust?

   _____

3. How does trust affect the economy?

   _____

4. What does it take to build trust?

   _____

   _____

5. What are the traits of the most trusted people in your organization? In your personal life?

   _____

   _____

6. How can you inspire trust in your organization?

   _____

   _____

Trust is **always** a risk.

*Chapter Three*

# Barriers to Overcome

## 1111

---

Only 38% of informed publics in the US trust businesses to do what is right. Only 49% of informed publics globally trust businesses.[1]

---

For any great mission it is valuable to know what you are up against. To gain *The Trust Edge,* there are some barriers to overcome, but I promise it is worth it. Trust has decreased significantly over recent years. A study by global market research company, Datamonitor, found that 86% of the consumers in the USA and Europe are less trusting of companies than they were just five years ago. Findings from a Watson Wyatt survey of 13,000 people in varied job levels and industries agree. According to their study, "Fewer than two out of five employees today have trust or confidence in their senior leaders."[2] While statistics like this may seem to paint a dim picture, we can change it. In order to overcome the barriers, let's first identify them. Once we know where they lie, we will overcome these barriers by using the Pillars that will be shared in Part II.

# Barrier #1: Conflicts of Interest

There are a multitude of conflicts of interest that create a lack of trust. Conflicts exist between venture capitalists and the long-term growth plan of an organization, shareholders and management, personal investors and banks, auditors and boards, teachers and parents, and politicians and the public, just to name a few. Take the venture capitalist whose goal is to make the company public and "cash in" quickly before it tanks. Or consider the politician in an economic downturn voting for a bill to give politicians a pay raise. For one government agency with whom I recently spoke and consulted, major trust issues stemmed from a disagreement between which agency, or portion of the agency, should get new environmental funding. Because of the conflict of interest, certain groups withheld valuable information from other groups. Trust was squandered, and the American people were not well served.

> More than two-thirds of people don't believe advertisers and marketing.[3] —Yankelovich study

# Barrier #2: Rising Litigation

In this high-litigation, prenuptial-focused culture, trust can stay shallow. People are worried about whom they can trust, or what someone might do to them if they make a mistake, even if it is unintentional.

# Barrier #3: Low Customer Loyalty

Years ago, Americans would buy Ford or Chevrolet all their lives because they thought it was important to be loyal. Not so today.

Customer loyalty is lower than ever. People don't think of being loyal. They think of themselves. People no longer feel loyalty from companies either. They may think, *Why be loyal to them when they have not been loyal to me?* In today's flat economy, relational depth is low, and access to the best deal is high. For instance, to buy an insurance product, I used to meet the sales person and establish a relationship before doing business. Today, quotes and policies are compared and bought online with no relationship. One can see how it takes work and trust to build real loyalty in today's climate.

## Barrier #4: Media Coverage of Scandals

Being bombarded with all the negative news coverage, whether accurate or exaggerated, often creates more negativity because it leaves the possibility in our minds. Many would not think another would do such a distrusting action until they hear that someone has indeed done such a thing. This in turn makes a person think someone might do that to them, and distrust abounds.

## Barrier #5: Speedy Social Networks

"What if this gets out?" "What if it gets spun the wrong way?" It can all happen in two clicks. Information, critiques, and recommendations travel quickly across social networks like Facebook and Twitter. Opinions that either build or destroy trust can make it around the world in no time.

## Barrier #6: Technology

The average person does not understand how it all works, and so technology can breed skepticism. "How did my computer get that virus?" "Is someone grabbing information off of my computer when I have it open?" Having to rely on someone else to diagnose all the specialized electronics in one's life can leave the consumer feeling out of control. Moreover, technology, though amazing, has failed nearly everyone. In one unfortunate power surge, we lost 22 devices, including appliances and computers. You don't realize how dependent you are on your appliances and computers until you lose ALL of them! For all of my childhood, we dialed the same beige rotary phone bound by a cord. That technology was king for years. Now it is hard to imagine owning the same cell phone for more than a couple of years. Because trust is built by consistency over time, rapidly changing technology can be a barrier.

## Barrier #7: Fear

Fear of the unknown is human and an obvious barrier to trust. We most easily trust the familiar. With such rapid change, there is so much to grasp. If we don't understand something, then it is hard to trust it.

---

"Fear will cause you to view things in such a twisted manner that you lose all healthy sense of perspective. Then you will doubt what you should trust and trust what you should doubt."[4] —Lisa Bevere, author

---

## Barrier #8: Negative Experiences

People have become more skeptical than ever. Recent studies show that 80% of Americans do not trust corporate leaders. Moreover, about half of all employees no longer trust their own managers.[5] When my brother walked into the parking lot after an NFL game, and someone put a gun to his head, took his keys, his money, and then his brand new car, he was forever changed. There are things he will never forget. And my brother's ability to trust certain people and places will be more difficult than the average person. If someone lost money on the Internet, it comes as no surprise that they will be less likely to trust online sites. If a woman was abused by a man, it is understandable that she will have a harder time trusting men in the future. With trust in business, negative experiences are a detriment.

---

Only 50% of young Americans—aged 15 to 25—trust the government to do the right thing most or some of the time.[6]

---

## Barrier #9: Individualism

In our culture, individualism is prized, and interdependence is under-valued. By nature individualism lacks a need, capacity, and desire to trust. While being able to do things on your own has its value, it can hurt our ability and genuine need to trust others. Interdependence means each is dependable and yet also depends on each other. To overcome this barrier, we must get rid of the arrogance that we know everything and can do everything on our own. We must think of the role and value of each individual as well as consider how we can better affect the greater good together. Remember the forest analogy? One of the reasons a Redwood forest is so strong is because the roots not only spread deep but also spread wide. They connect and weave together to form an even stronger network of roots. It is the same with trust. We are our own trees but are strengthened enormously by being connected with others.

## Barrier #10: Diverse Thinking

Certainly there is value in diversity of thoughts, ideas, and cultures. However, people are, and always have been, fearful of the unknown. Harvard Political Scientist Robert Putnam's epic study on diversity revealed a surprising finding. Based on detailed interviews of nearly 30,000 people across America he found, "In the most diverse communities, neighbors trust one another about half as much as they do in the most homogenous settings."[7]

This is why some organizations find that although diversity leads to innovation, creativity, and success in many ways, it also can be a barrier to trust. People most quickly trust the familiar. People prefer to work with someone in whom they can find commonality. Do we share values, they wonder? Differing views can make for lack of unity. In that way diversity can create a barrier when trying to build trust. Though difference of thought and background can be an obstacle, we will see that deep trust can become vibrant in spite of this barrier.

## Barrier #11: Instant Gratification

In today's world people want everything fast, without effort, discipline, or hard work. In this time of email, self-check-out lines, digital cameras, instant news, easy-access music, and same-day delivery, speed has become an expectation. Trust can take work and time. For this reason it may be unachieved. Still, there is no other way to sustained success but to be trusted.

## Barrier #12: Focus on the Negative

Another difficulty in understanding trust is that much of the research around trust has traditionally focused on how trust has been ruined rather than how it can be built. In her research on trust, author Janet Presser concurs, "We know more about how to destroy trust than we know how to build it."[8]

Now it is time to solve the trust problem. What many need is a clear way to build trust. There is hope, even for those who have broken trust.

# Barriers to Overcome

¶ For any great mission it is worth knowing what you are up against.

¶ In most sectors, trust has decreased significantly in recent years.

¶ The barriers to overcome include:

1. Conflicts of interest

2. Rising litigation

3. Lower customer loyalty

4. Media coverage of scandals

5. Word of mouth/social networks

6. Technology

7. Fear

8. Negative experiences

9. Individualism

10. Diverse thinking

11. Instant gratification

12. Focus on the negative

## Ask Yourself ...

1. What destroys trust?

   _____

   _____

2. What barriers do you come up against the
   most often?

   _____

   _____

   _____

3. What barriers are most important for you to
   overcome?

   _____

   _____

4. How might you start to overcome these
   barriers?

   _____

   _____

   _____

   _____

   _____

   _____

# PART II
## THE
## EIGHT PILLARS
## OF TRUST

Trust is the natural result of thousands of tiny actions, words, thoughts, and intentions. It doesn't happen by accident, nor does it happen all at once. Gaining trust is work. Knowing that you need it isn't enough; you and I have to do the little things on a daily basis to earn it.

In the following chapters, you will find not only the Eight Pillars of Trust, attributes that put leaders like Warren Buffett and companies like Google on top, but also practical ways to put that information immediately to use.

Some of the key traits of the trusted could fit under more than one pillar. For instance, listening is one of the best ways to show Compassion (Pillar 2) and is also a major part of Connection (Pillar 6). Instead of overlapping, I highlighted the trait in the chapter that fit best. Let's get to the Pillars.

People trust
the clear
and distrust
the ambiguous.

*Chapter Four*

# Pillar One:
# Clarity

∩∩∩∩

---

"Stick to what you know." —Warren Buffett

---

Without a clear plan, employees are confused and become ineffective. Without a clear product choice, prospects won't buy. It's difficult to have faith in someone who has fuzzy plans or unclear expectations. People trust the clear and distrust the ambiguous. Confusion breeds fear, frustration, and lack of focus.

For the trusted leader, clarity starts with honesty. In an extensive study by Forum Corporation, hundreds of salespeople from 11 companies in five industries were investigated. The aim was to find the difference between top producers and average ones. The fascinating results revealed that the difference was not charisma, ability, or knowledge. The unique trait of top producers was nothing other than honesty! Honest communicators build trust.[1]

Clarity is also increased when a message is heard or seen frequently. According to one significant global survey, people need to hear information about a company three to five times in order to believe that the information is credible.[2] In order to establish clarity, make sure the communication is honest and repeated.

## Three Key Areas of Clarity

In your quest for *The Trust Edge*, clarity has three different and equally important areas for the trusted leader:

1. Vision and Purpose.

2. Expectations and Communications.

3. Daily Tasks.

## Clarity, Part I:
# Vision and Purpose

"Without vision people perish."[3]—Solomon, King of Israel (970-928 BC)

## Don't be like Orville

I met an 88-year-old man named Orville at my health club, first noticing him one afternoon while checking in. I saw Orville sort of stumbling along behind me. I couldn't believe my eyes. There was no way this man, slowly shuffling along the path to the gym, was going to work out! Orville patiently moved, inch by inch, into the weight-training area, picked up some dumbbells, and with an audible grunt, started his routine.

PART I

CLARITY

COMPASSION

CHARACTER

COMPETENCY

COMMITMENT

CONNECTION

CONTRIBUTION

CONSISTENCY

PART III

PART IV

PART V

Then one day I happened to see him out of the corner of my eye stepping onto one of the treadmills. I was across the room, and he was already reaching for the start button. Too far away to help him, I just stood there and watched. As the treadmill came to life, Orville took one small step, and then another. The machine picked up speed, but miraculously, so did his legs. Within a minute, he hit full stride, running like a man half his age!

At this point, the reality of the situation dawned on me. Orville's problem wasn't with his legs, it was with his vision. He couldn't see where he was going. He shuffled along slowly, not because he couldn't run, but because he was worried that he would knock his knee, shin, or toe on the nearest weight equipment.

Though Orville did nothing to cause his vision problem, it is a powerful example of how limited we are when we lack clarity and vision. Being capable, but having no vision is poor stewardship. We, as individuals and organizations, can't afford that. Without clarity, speed and meaningful action are impossible. With clear focus we not only become more efficient and effective, but we also build trust.

Helen Keller, the first deaf-blind person to earn a Bachelor of Arts degree, said, "The most pathetic person in the world is someone who has sight, but has no vision."

## Vision Impacts Everything

Few things inspire trust or hope like every member of a team working together towards a shared vision. A clear vision unifies and motivates. We see it in sports all the time. Certain teams, often lacking a big-name super star, seem to "gel" or "come together" at just the right moment. Often, when interviewed after the game, the players will comment on how focused they were on the common goal. When the players understand their role as well as the larger strategy and vision, the ground is fertile for success to grow.

Vision impacts the way we work in every imaginable way, from how we answer the phone to the way we describe our job, because it affects the way we feel about those things. People do small, even menial tasks differently when they catch a great vision. If you are a leader in your organization, share your vision consistently. If you are not sharing your vision at least every thirty days, your team doesn't know it. A clear vision inspires, unifies, and gives powerful focus. That is why I'm always disheartened when I travel to a company and learn that no one can tell me about their organization's vision or mission.

---

Leading industry analysts estimate that 95% of workers are unaware of their company's top objectives.[4]

---

## Clouded Visions

Vision can get a bad rap. It's often used as a kind of soft metaphor, something to talk about when you don't have a concrete strategy in place. This is selling the concept short. Vision isn't a replacement for strategy; it's the reason you have one.

A few years into my tenure as a young director of the youth and family development organization, K-Life, Inc., things were going well. I was doing work I was passionate about while enjoying a great staff and board of directors. Even though there was great fulfill-ment in my job, my wife and I felt the burning desire to start our own business. We decided to pack up and head back to family in Minnesota. It wasn't easy to leave behind the security of a good job at an organization we loved, but we felt deeply that it was the right decision.

All of the sudden we had no salary, no benefits, no company car, and no place to live. Even the clearest of visions can be clouded by difficult circumstances. I'll never forget the summer evening we sat on the curb next to a grocery store. We sat together, my arm around my wife while she cried, because we didn't have enough money for food. By October of that year, we had thrown everything we had into that new business. After paying our urgent bills, we only had $1.40 split between two bank accounts—80 cents in one account and 60 cents in the other account. We lived in a musty basement apartment with no windows. Although we needed to go upstairs to share a bathroom and kitchen with the landlady, we were grateful. We had a vision of what could be, a vision that wouldn't be removed with a tinge of hardship. That vision kept us unified and focused even when things were not easy.

I remember when I considered taking on a part-time job to make ends meet. During that time, I received some bold and wise advice from my brother. His perspective was crystal clear. "Don't take the job," he told me. "If you take a side job, you won't need to build this business. And if you don't *need* to, you won't." This may not be true for every circumstance, but deep down, I knew he was right, so I kept pouring everything I had into the business.

We are grateful for God's provision through that time. Our company, Special Delivery Productions, was involved in performing, producing, and sharing positive messages at big events across the

PART I
CLARITY
COMPASSION
CHARACTER
COMPETENCY
COMMITMENT
CONNECTION
CONTRIBUTION
CONSISTENCY
PART III
PART IV
PART V

country. By the end of our first year, we had contracts for events in places as far away as Japan. Am I ever grateful for the vision we had that kept us unified, focused, and motivated!

## Do One or Two Things Well

"Success demands singleness of purpose."
—Vincent Lombardi, ESPN's Coach of the Century

Having one or two specialties in which you excel is important. It signals to clients that you know what you're doing, and you're going to be competent in your specialty area instead of trying to be all things to all people. This goes a long way toward establishing trust. A family physician who knows his strengths and limitations will surely gain *The Trust Edge* with his patients, if he is confident about his diagnoses and treatment plans, yet willing to refer the patient to a specialist when the condition goes beyond the scope of his knowledge.

Consider the clarity gap of these two companies. Kmart and Walmart both opened their first store in 1962 with similar visions for discount stores. Kmart was clearly the market leader. But Kmart got distracted. They made acquisitions, such as Waldenbooks and Sports Authority, that were irrelevant to their central vision. Kmart's strength was diluted and Walmart became the discount powerhouse.[5]

"Keep growing your core business; beware the unfamiliar."[6]
—Richard P. Chapman, Professor of Business Administration

## Clarity, the Secret to Google's Success

Google has become the web user's favorite search engine. Type a term or phrase in the Google box and following is a list of sites containing relevant information. Google wasn't the first search engine to enter the market, and yet, they have climbed their way up to the dominant position with 80% of the market share and a hefty $21 billion revenue.[7] All of this success comes despite being a little more than an idea just 10 years ago. So how did Google get to be so big, so fast?

It can be traced back to the clarity of their vision. Google's mission is simple: "To organize the world's information and make it universally accessible and useful."[8] This includes everything from the company's magnificently simple home page to the complicated algorithm that generates results. Google is enjoying the public's trust as well as huge profits.

---

"The secret to success is constancy of purpose."—Benjamin Disraeli

---

## Clarity of Message

Sweden's Ingvar Kamprad didn't start out to be a furniture mogul. When Kamprad was a young boy in Sweden in the 1930s, he realized that he could buy matches in Stockholm at wholesale prices, and then sell them to his neighbors at a discounted price while still making a profit. Soon his business expanded to include Christmas decorations, seeds, pens and pencils—all of which he literally pedaled door to door on a bicycle. Kamprad's father gave him money as a reward for his success in school. Ingvar Kamprad saved and used the

PART I

CLARITY

COMPASSION

CHARACTER

COMPETENCY

COMMITMENT

CONNECTION

CONTRIBUTION

CONSISTENCY

PART III

PART IV

PART V

money in 1943 to begin a retail business named IKEA. The company at first sold a mix of smaller household items such as picture frames, wallets, and even nylon stockings, with some locally manufactured furniture. Most of the sales were mail order, although Kamprad would occasionally still make house visits. Whatever Kamprad had to sell, though, he had the clear and simple goal of selling quality goods to his customers at a discounted price.

Smaland, the area of Sweden that Kamprad was raised in, is known for hard-working, frugal people, and Ingvar Kamprad is one of their best ambassadors. The word *frugal* is often misrepresented to mean "cheap," but if you have ever met a frugal person, you would know the difference. A frugal person may buy a high-ticket item, not because of the status, but because he believes he won't need to buy again for a very long time. Frugal people aren't against spending money; they simply don't like wasting it. They also don't like to waste materials or time. Kamprad remained guided by his Smalander principles for his entire life.

By 1953, IKEA clarified their line by exclusively selling furniture, and opened a showroom in Amhult, Sweden, so the customers could inspect the furniture before they bought it. This was apparently a successful idea, because by 1955, Kamprad's furniture manufacturers were boycotting him because of pressure from his competitors. At this point, Kamprad could have raised his prices, lowered the quality of his furniture, or even started selling automobiles. Kamprad decided to stick with furniture, however, and renewed his determination to keep low prices and high-quality products. Success struck again when storage issues drove the company to create furniture that could be stored flat and assembled by consumers.

Since its founding in 1943, IKEA has doubled in size every four years. By 1978, they had stores in Switzerland, Germany, Canada, the United States, Japan, Hong Kong, Singapore, and Australia. IKEA's loyal, worldwide following all began with Kamprad's clear vision of bringing quality goods to the public at discounted prices.[9]

## The Oracle of Omaha

Born in 1930 to middle-class parents in Omaha, Nebraska, Warren Buffett has become one of the richest men in the world because of his stock market investment strategies. His apparent wisdom has earned him the nickname, "The Oracle of Omaha." Many individuals and groups have made timely investment decisions because of Buffett. Considered by many to be the most trusted businessman in the world, his success has been unmatched.[10]

When working with stocks, it is common for investors, and sometimes for investment brokers, to become enamored with a particular company or industry. Once a person has an emotional stake in a particular company, they can lose their objectivity about the long-term prospects for that company. In contrast, Buffett's approach to investment is based on clear common sense. He calculates the actual worth of the company in question and compares that worth to its presumed worth on the stock market. If the company is undervalued, he buys the stock. If the company is overvalued, Buffet either doesn't buy it or sells the stock if he owns it.

As a consequence of his success, many investors hang on every pronouncement that Buffett makes. His followers have come to trust that Buffett does not get sidetracked by trends or emotions while investing. Buffett's consistent performance and clear purpose have made him, and many other people, a great deal of money.

## This Media Knows Its Market

The Cable Satellite Public Affairs Network (C-SPAN), nearly 30 years old, isn't the television station to tune into for political fluff. Nor does it fill the airwaves with the new style of media journalism that some describe as mere editorial opinion disguised as news. Viewers won't find competitive taglines or shouts of clever advertising jargon. That vein of political entertainment is found on the other television news channels. Yet C-SPAN and its staff have garnered a long list of awards. They run the gamut, from the *Peabody* to the *Golden Beacon* to the *Presidential Medal of Freedom*.

C-SPAN, the brainchild of Chairman and CEO Brian Lamb, has one primary mission: to provide public access to the political process. Their goals are clear, and although they have expanded their programming menu since 1979, it never deviates from its original mission.

They operate on the premise that citizens inherently want to trust that the information being broadcasted is unfiltered and unedited, spoken directly to them from the house floor, without the color commentary. C-SPAN has achieved exemplary trust through their famous brand of transparency and clarity.[11]

---

"Great leaders are almost always great simplifiers
who can cut through the argument, debate, and doubt
to offer a solution everybody can understand." —Colin Powell

---

## The Paradox of Choice

We Americans love choice, autonomy, and freedom...at least we think we love it. But too much choice actually inhibits happiness, says Professor Barry Schwartz, who coined the term "the paradox of choice."[12]

Shop for jeans, and there's boot cut, easy cut, slim cut, this cut, and that cut. Having an overload of choices creates unrealistically high expectations (i.e., the perfect-fitting pair of jeans) causes you to question decisions after you make them, and sets up self-blame and failure. (What if I missed something better?)

One store set up two times where its clientele could taste-test jam for free. The first time, 24 flavors were offered; the second time, 6 flavors were offered.

Clients could try as many as they wished. Interestingly, both times people tasted the same amount of jam. When 24 jams were available, only 3 percent of the people bought a jar of jam. When 6 jams were available, 30 percent bought a jar of jam.[13]

Some organizations are very successful because they offer limited choices. An average grocery store has 40,000 items; Costco has 4,000 items. Yet studies show Costo shoppers leave the happiest— even when they have far less to choose from.[14]

In the push toward clarity, narrow your organization's choices to a few good things, with specific groups in mind. Create binary decision-making. Ask, "Do you want a 4-door or a 2-door car?" Then, "Do you want one that operates on gas, or a hybrid?" Suddenly, it's not only easy for your clients to choose, but they'll have a better, less stressful experience—and will come back because they walk away, happy and satisfied.

## A Mission Statement Improves Clarity

A simple mission statement gives clarity of purpose. I have one for my company, my family, and my personal life. In each case the mission statement gives me direction and helps guide my priorities.

Early on in the life of our business, my wife and I sat down and composed our first mission statement. Our mission—*To share life-changing truth in a unique and impacting way*—became a guide for every decision. This simple vision has helped guide booking decisions, hiring decisions, and the generation of new material. It keeps us focused on doing "best" activities rather than just "good" things. It is very easy to get caught up in doing things that are good but not necessarily the best use of our time or talents. All of my writing, consulting, speaking, and resources are aimed toward making an impact in my area of expertise. With a clear focus, a bigger difference is made.

Our family has developed a mission statement along with twelve tenets that guide the operations of our family. What happens? We know who we are and have become more unified and intentional. I also have a personal mission statement above my desk—as does my wife and my staff. Why create a personal mission statement? You will become more accountable, more focused, and more motivated. If you would like to see how to create a mission statement for yourself, your family, or your business, feel free to visit our resource site, www.TheTrustEdge.com.

## Clarity, Part II:
# Expectation & Communication

### Expectations

Few things are as frustrating as working for a manager who gives you an annual review and tells you all the things she thinks you should have been doing during the past year. How is this information helpful now? The year is over. Why weren't these expectations expressed *earlier*? If you are a parent, you know how important it is to communicate expectations with your child. So often, a clear communication of expectations will prevent both misbehavior and failure.

As little sense as it makes, I hear about similar situations all the time. Supervisors need to be clear about their expectations. This is true in my own company. When I'm specific with my requests about what I want, I almost always receive what I asked for. When I'm vague in my requests, I typically receive something other than what I had in mind.

If you're in charge of leading your group or even a company, consider whether you're communicating specific expectations effectively. Of course, micromanagement is a supreme trust killer, not to mention a spectacular waste of time. But in most cases, if you are clear about the outcome in mind, it will get done, sometimes even beyond your expectations.

My new marketing director was feeling overwhelmed and losing motivation. I could see it. When I inquired, she said she felt like there was so much to do but didn't know what to do first. Once we clarified priorities and expectations, her motivation, effectiveness, and enthusiasm returned. As her leader, helping her work through this was my responsibility.

If you work for someone who is vague about what they want, spend a few minutes talking with him or her about your work. Find out expectations, including the appropriate deadlines and priorities. If it isn't possible to finish everything on your plate at once, figure out what's most important. You'll foster greater trust and a more productive workplace at the same time.

# Be Candid

Part of being clear is being transparent and authentic. Mean what you say and say what you mean. Share the truth. The trusted are candid; they aren't afraid to tell the truth in the clearest terms possible. When people appear to be hiding something, we worry about what it could be and lose confidence. In the interview process, if an applicant hesitates or gives excuses for why he cannot provide references, then that is a red flag. On the other hand, if without a pause, the applicant is quick to give several names, phone numbers, and a bit about their relationship, then it seems references hardly need to be checked. Appearing to hide something breeds skepticism. Secrets destroy trust. Being candid, whether it is during hard economic conditions or during a new project, puts your staff on the same page and builds trust. Yes, being confidential about appropriate matters is important, but when you are willing to share relevant information, people feel trusted and are more apt to give you the benefit of the doubt.

Most of us want to be liked. And so, there is always a temptation to water down what we say so as to be careful with sensitive people. At the same time, recognize that people can't put their faith in you if they know you're going to take the easy way out. Candidness implies giving bad news when appropriate, even though you know it could hurt. It means giving honest assessments when they're called for. Just as you should make a point to appreciate people when you catch them doing something great, you must be quick to address issues candidly. Some managers withhold bad news because they are more worried about being liked than dealing with issues that affect everyone. I have seen managers go through tough financial times. The ones who are frank and transparent become trusted, and the team, in spite of uncertain times, remains unified. Authenticity and frankness inspire.

> "Corporations from CEOs down must stay in close touch with stakeholders, respond quickly to questions, and get out any changed circumstances or bad news as it develops."[15]
> —Doug Schoen, author, pollster, and advisor to President Clinton

In my consultation work with a tech firm, I became aware of a top manager who was coming in late, going home early, and not taking responsibility for his job. That manager was given fewer and fewer projects, and people started to resent that a highly paid manager could get away with such slacking behavior. The vice president over this man would not hold him accountable for his actions.

Two devastating things happened. People resented the lazy manager, as you might expect. More importantly, they lost trust in the vice president, who was unwilling to address the problem. Sadly, morale tanked, and this tech firm lost *The Trust Edge*. I have seen this avoidance of the truth kill morale and productivity many times. Is there a place where you or your team needs to be more straightforward in your communication with clients or colleagues?

> "Only with transparent policies will it be possible for government to regain the confidence of the European public."[16]
> —Antonio Martins de la Cruz, former Foreign Affairs Minister of Portugal

## Shared Meanings = Clear Communication

People in organizations typically spend over 75% of their time in an interpersonal situation; thus it is no surprise to find that at the root of a large number of organizational problems is poor communication.[15]

> "Social psychologists estimate that there is usually a 40-60% loss of meaning in the transmission of messages from sender to receiver."[17]

**Communication is shared meaning.** To the extent that one shares meaning with another, the two parties communicated. Anyone familiar with the academic side of communication can tell you, it's very difficult for any two people, much less groups, to accurately convey meaning to one another. Our minds are too filled with our own assumptions. For example, suppose I asked you to think of a person riding a horse. Some of you, by virtue of your background or imagination, might picture a cowboy galloping through the mountains. Others of you might instinctively envision a girl, jumping gates in an arena. Your mind's eye colors things differently than others based on your experiences.

> No two people ever perfectly communicate. However, the more clearly we communicate, the greater the ability to trust.

Clear communication is difficult for another reason. Some studies suggest that over 90% of the meaning we derive comes from nonverbal cues that one person gives to another.[18] That means only 10% of communication is based on words we say! Clear communication is work.

> "The vision is really about empowering workers, giving them all the information about what's going on so they can do a lot more than they've done in the past."
>
> —Bill Gates, Chairman of Microsoft Corporation

PART I

CLARITY

COMPASSION

CHARACTER

COMPETENCY

COMMITMENT

CONNECTION

CONTRIBUTION

CONSISTENCY

PART III

PART IV

PART V

---

**Clear Communicators**

- Listen.

- Empathize.

- Avoid manipulation. Don't overstate or understate.

- Speak honestly and without exaggeration.

- Stay focused and avoid distractions.

- Ask questions.

- Glean information from the nonverbal communication.

- Keep an open mind and do not jump to conclusions.

- Do not criticize.

- Simplify the complicated.

- First seek to understand, and then to be understood.

- Mean what they say.

---

## Conflict is Inevitable!

Most conflict occurs because of a lack of clarity in communication, so I feel it is important to address here. Expect conflict. Learn to deal with it. Anytime there's more than one person, you're bound to find conflict. It's only natural. We all have separate backgrounds, different tendencies, and unique perspectives. It's no surprise we disagree from time to time. I am always amazed at the splits in friendships, churches, and businesses over a little conflict. Who do you agree with 100% of the time? Nobody. I don't even agree with those I love the most, all of the time. Have you noticed how people will escalate in their friendship as long as they are talking about commonalities? However, when differences are found, the energy and engagement often drops. We may agree on many things, but now that I know you voted for one person and I voted for another, we can hardly be friends. Don't let it happen. Expect and even appreciate conflict. The old notion rings true that if we are all exactly the same we are not all needed. Conflict can be a source of growth, creativity, and in the end, greater unity.

**Constructive Conflict**

- *The key to conflict is not avoiding it;* it's dealing with it effectively.

- *Conflict is inevitable and necessary for improvement.* We can't grow if we're never challenged, so get used to seeing conflict as a way to spur positive change, not an attack on your point of view.

- *Use it as a chance to gather information.* Understand that conflict resolution often gives the chance to gather input and clarify expectations.

- *Ask "Why?"* Often, the best way out of conflict is to keep asking "Why?" The root of the problem might not be apparent on the surface.

- *Practice empathy.* There's no better remedy for a disagreement than putting yourself in someone else's shoes. Pause and be open to the other's point of view and reasoning.

- *Stick to the facts.* Don't focus on negative feelings or perceived intentions, but rather, concentrate on what happened, and what you can do about it.

- *Practice using "I" language.* Using "You" language like, "You always," or "I wish you wouldn't do that" puts the other person on the defensive. "I thought this," or "I felt this way," allows you to express yourself more clearly and helps the other person better appreciate your point of view.

> "Conflicts don't arise without a cause,
> and don't disappear until the cause is addressed."
> —Florence Stone, management expert and author

## Clarity, Part III:
# Daily Tasks

While I agree with Ben Franklin's idea, "If you fail to plan, you plan to fail," countless companies have wasted time and money on strategic plans that are collecting dust. People spend lots of time planning but very little time turning those plans into daily actionable tasks. Some suggest that putting your goal in the mirror so you see it every day will make it come true. I would suggest that your mission statement belongs on your mirror, and your goals and tasks associated with achieving your mission are meant for action. Daily clarity leads to accomplishing the most important things every day. I will give my Difference Making Action (DMA) method for having daily clarity in Chapter 10, the Contribution Chapter. DMAs are the best way I have found to be clear on a daily basis. They will keep you from having a day where you feel like you are busy but getting nothing done. For this chapter, I offer a similar idea that may prove helpful.

The following idea comes from Charles Schwab, the first American to be paid a million dollar salary.

In the early 1900s Schwab was President of the Bethlehem Steel Company. The small steel company was struggling. A business consultant named Ivy Lee told Schwab that he could share in 15 minutes a strategy with Schwab's managers that would double productivity. When Schwab inquired about the price for the help, Lee said, "After using it for six months, you can pay me what you think it's worth."

Here's what Ivy Lee told Charles Schwab and his managers: "Every night, at the end of each day, write down the six most important things that need to get done the next day. Write only six, no more. Prioritize them with number one being the most important. In the morning, start with number one and do only number one until it is completed. Do not go on to number 2 until number one is completed. When number one

> **Apply It!**
> To create laser focus and clarity you may need to let go of some distractions. Ask yourself:
> - ❑ What tasks or projects do we have that fall outside our mission or core business?
> - ❑ What activities are holding us back from greater success?
> - ❑ Am I doing any "good" things that are keeping me from doing the "best" things?

is completed go on to number 2, then do only number 2 until it is completed. And so on. If you get done with all of them you can start a new list."

Only a few months passed when Mr. Lee received a letter from the Bethlehem Steel Company. Inside the envelope, Mr. Lee found a check in the amount of $25,000 ($250,000 in today's dollars) and a note from Schwab saying the lesson was the most profitable he had ever learned. The voluntary payment to Mr. Lee was quite a bargain considering that Bethlehem Steel went on to become one of the giants in the steel industry and one of the most successful corporations in U.S. history.[19]

# Pillar One: Clarity

❡ Clarity unifies, motivates, increases morale, and inspires trust. Clear communication leads to trusted colleagues and happy employees.

❡ People trust the clear, and distrust the vague.

❡ Clarity can reduce conflict within your staff and with customers.

❡ The trusted are candid and are not afraid to tell the truth.

❡ Leaders need to share the vision at least every 30 days.

❡ Clarity gives focus on daily actionable tasks.

❡ Learn to let go.

❡ Ask managers for input and clarity of expectations frequently.

¶ Specificity is a motivator.

¶ People can't do a great job if they don't understand expectations.

¶ Communication is "shared meaning."

¶ The key to conflict is not in avoiding it altogether, but in dealing with it effectively.

## Ask Yourself ...

1. Do you know your company's mission or vision? Is there clarity of purpose?

   _____

   _____

   _____

2. Do you give clear and specific expectations for projects and deadlines?

   _____

3. How could you be clearer in your communication with others?

   _____

   _____

   _____

4. Do you avoid conflict and confrontation? If so, how do you get things resolved?

   _____

   _____

   _____

   _____

5. Are you clear about your own daily tasks?

   _____

A clear vision
unifies and
motivates.

"If you find it
in your heart to
care for somebody else,
you will have
succeeded."

—Maya Angelou
American autobiographer and poet

*Chapter Five*

# Pillar Two:
# Compassion

Who do you trust more, firefighters or mortgage brokers? Librarians or lawyers? Nurses or salespeople? One of the biggest reasons for trust is the perception that someone is concerned beyond themselves for the good of the whole. Firefighters and nurses care for others by nature of their jobs. But we wonder if the salesperson really has our best interest in mind. Don't worry if you are in a less trusted line of work. Resolve to be among the trusted in your field. Show that you think beyond yourself; you will be unique and successful in your industry.

Do not underestimate the bottom-line impact of compassion. The ability to show care, empathy, and compassion is a heavy component of trust. The ability is rooted in two long-standing virtues. The first is being able to "walk in someone else's shoes" and understand things from his or her experience. The second is continually acting out, "Do unto others as you would have them do unto you." On a basic level, the link between care and trust is fundamental. The aphorism is true: "Nobody cares how much you know until they know how much you care."

Though Milton Freidman famously claimed in 1970 that the social responsibility of business is to increase profits, things have changed. Forty years later people want to do business with those who have concern for the whole of humanity. President and CEO of the world's largest independent PR firm and trust researcher, Richard Edelman noted, "We've moved from a shareholder to a stakeholder world in which business must recast its role to act in the public's interest as well as for private gain."[2] Even Adam Smith, the father of modern economics, acknowledged that the ultimate goal of business is not to make a profit. "Profit is the reward one gets for serving the general welfare," according to Author and Professor Walter Wink.[3] No matter your profession, challenge yourself to start thinking like the customer, patient, client, congregation member, or student. Think of their needs and their challenges. Care about THEM. Give them a great experience. Make them feel valued. Not only is it fun and self-gratifying, but it will also help you gain *The Trust Edge*.

---

"We need to use dignity as the guiding principle for all actions."[4]

—H.R.H. Crown Prince Haakon of Norway

---

## The Most Trusted Person in the World

Although teachers and doctors tend to be the most trusted professionals, there is nobody more trusted than a mom. Very, very few people trust anyone more than their mother. Why? Because they have learned from experience that Mom thinks beyond herself. In most cases she is committed to her children like no one else. She wants the best for her children in every area of their lives, and will do anything to both protect and provide for them. Mom will sacrifice. Sometimes that means staying up late to help with homework. Other times it means making favorite foods or the midnight soothing of a sick stomach. I am grateful for my caring, sacrificing mother. I know not everyone has this. But for most, when things get tough, Mom is always there. Magazines and news shows are rife with examples of single mothers who will work multiple jobs, foregoing their own health and happiness, just to give their kids the best possible chance at life. When it comes to building *The Trust Edge* through compassion, commitment, and sacrifice, mothers are at the top!

## Starbucks Brews Up Employee Loyalty

Time and again, workers have shown that they are more apt to stay put when they feel like their company cares for them. A study conducted by the Saratoga Institute in California, considered by many to be the leader in exit-interview surveying, revealed that 89% of managers believed that most employees left for better pay. Yet when the group polled employees who left their companies voluntarily, they found that nearly the exact same amount of workers (88%) actually cited something other than salary as the main motivation for the switch.[5] A Gallup report found that "employees don't leave companies, they leave managers and supervisors."[6] People leave because they are

PART I

CLARITY

COMPASSION

CHARACTER

COMPETENCY

COMMITMENT

CONNECTION

CONTRIBUTION

CONSISTENCY

PART III

PART IV

PART V

not respected, listened to, appreciated, or cared about. People who are cared for have a hard time leaving, even for more money. Not only is caring the right thing to do, but attrition caused by reckless lack of concern is costly. Increasing retention of both customers and employees is one of the best ways to boost the bottom line.

The gold standard of business in this area of retention is Starbucks. By providing benefits like health care and retirement options to the majority of their employees, even part-timers, they've created a culture of loyalty within their organization that is largely unmatched by their competitors. The giant coffee chain employs more than 80,000 in the U.S. alone, and currently spends more on benefits than they do on coffee beans and other raw materials. At the same time, they enjoy a low turnover rate of around 16% for full-time employees, compared to a 300% average within the fast-food industry.[7] By showing employees they care, they don't just get better effort, they save millions on training and recruitment.

> "A caring company structure was a primary factor in producing superior results."[8] —Nohria Nitin, William Joyce, and Bruce Robertson, study of 200 management practices

## The Leader that Made Compassionate Cola

Growing up in Madras, India, Indra Nooyi had always dreamed of living in the United States. It started when she came to the U.S. to earn her M.B.A. from Yale in 1978. She joined PepsiCo in 1994. In 2006 Nooyi became CEO of PepsiCo and has since led the mega-brand that is in nearly 200 countries. Her legacy is that of compassion with an eye on the bottom line. Her motto: *Performance with purpose.* She shares her vision by saying, "We bring together what is good for business with what is good for the world." How has she built the Pillar of Compassion that has changed the bottom line?

- When Nooyi was awarded the CEO position in a race with a long-time colleague, she immediately flew out to meet the colleague and asked what she could do to keep him. She nearly matched her salary, among other things, and a great team was born.

- Nooyi made a commitment to move away from unhealthy food and drinks. Examples in the works are high-fiber oatmeal and low-calorie Gatorade. According to Michael Useem, "By 2010, Nooyi has pledged, half of Pepsi's US revenue will come from healthful foods."

- Nooyi has championed moves toward renewable energy and has campaigned against obesity.

What has happened because of decisions made by the lady known as the "Caring CEO"? Profits have soared. And so has influence and impact of the $39 billion PepsiCo.[9]

## The Four LAWS of Compassion

There are four key ways we show we care. I call them the LAWS of Compassion. They are four actions that we can use to show care and compassion in the workplace and in our homes: Listen, Appreciate, Wake up, and Serve others.

# "L" stands for Listen

The best way to show that you care is to really listen to people.

Growing up on the farm as the youngest of six kids, I learned how to eat fast, talk fast, and interrupt my siblings. Listening has not always come easily to me, and I'm not alone. Listening is a fundamental skill of genuine success, and it's hard to be great or trusted without it. The benefits of listening include more trust, better understanding, stronger marriages, happier kids, and increased respect at work. Still, being a good listener is hard work!

I learned a great lesson while talking with one of my closest friends. He was telling me about something troubling him in a hallway during the lunch hour. Several people passed by us, stopping to say hello along the way. Each time, even as my friend continued talking, I would look up and speak a friendly greeting. Finally, after a few of these interruptions, my friend simply stopped talking and said, "You don't care. You are not listening to what I am saying." What he said permanently changed my outlook on listening. He was absolutely right, and I knew it immediately. Rather than focus on his words, I was showing him he wasn't worthy of my attention. Bad listening habits aren't just rude; they are expensive. To this day, I'm grateful for his candor, because listening is such an important factor in *The Trust Edge*.

## My First Boardroom

I will never forget being in the boardroom for a staff meeting at one of my first jobs. The meeting was supposed to be an opportunity to deal with new business, talk through current issues, and raise any concerns. During the meeting I got a firsthand look at the impact listening has on personal trust and credibility. The board director, brilliant in many parts of running an organization, was wrapping up the session. With everything else on the agenda complete, he asked if there was anything else to discuss. Before anyone could answer, he turned his back to the staff, left the room, and let the door slam shut behind him. All the faces in the room were full of disbelief. I knew there were some who wanted to discuss a specific problem. The director lost his team that day. The director was competent and committed to his job but was not fully trusted. An unwillingness to listen is one of the fastest trust killers.

### Listening with a Narrow Focus

Naturally, for the best listeners, trust is increased exponentially. During college I spent one summer working as an intern for a trader on the floor of the Minneapolis Grain Exchange. In that fast-pace, high-pressure environment, fortunes can be gained and lost in seconds. In fact, with so much going on, you could imagine how difficult it would be to listen to anyone. But one man didn't see it that way. Instead of being caught up in the commotion going on around him, he made a concentrated effort to narrow his attention to whomever he was dealing with. It made no difference if he was speaking to another trader, the governor, or a floor clerk intern like me. When he spoke to someone, he wouldn't allow any interruptions. If he was on his phone, he didn't hold other conversations. One of his mantras was, "If you want to show someone you don't care, just use call waiting."

That kind of behavior is unusual in any field, especially his. But then again, so were his results. In just a few short years, he went from being a new trader at the Minneapolis Grain Exchange to Chairman of the Board at the Exchange. Eventually, he moved into even bigger realms, becoming CEO of the 500-member Exchange and later beginning other fruitful ventures. Success is never as simple as picking up one habit from a book. This man worked hard and had a dogged sense of preparation. However, he owes a great deal of his success to his ability to focus on listening to the person right in front of him.

---

**Tips for Effective Listening**

(When done genuinely and appropriately, the following will increase communication and trust.)

- *Keep eye contact.* Look at the person talking. You'll have an easier time paying attention, and they'll be grateful for your focus.

- *Listen with your body.* Nod and gesture with your hands to show you're keyed in to what the other person is saying. Make sure your posture and movements don't suggest you're bored or restless.

- *Practice patience.* When someone is speaking to you, resist the urge to have something ready to say in return. Listen carefully to what they're saying before answering.

- *Empathize.* Listening isn't just about the message. Intent and context are important, so try to make a habit of seeing things from their point of view. Try to really put your feet in the speaker's shoes. Avoid comments like, "I totally understand what you are going through."

---

> No one completely understands what someone else is going through. When we acknowledge that fact, our credibility as a listener goes way up.
>
> - *Be present.* Ask, "Am I present in this conversation?" Keep your focus on track.
>
> - *Avoid answering the electronic interrupter.* The phone, PDA, or email can be a useful means of communication. But if you are with someone, taking an interruption is one of the fastest ways to show you don't really care about him or her.
>
> - *Hold one conversation at a time.*

## A Gutsy VP Asks for Input

I consulted recently for a $40 billion health care company that was going through significant restructuring. The vice president was a brilliant leader, though his team occasionally saw him as aloof or distant on matters they cared about. I was given the task of talking with his 30-member team about how to regain and strengthen trust within the group and towards the leader. He needed me to gather and listen to their feedback if he was going to build trust in his organization. He left the room with this instruction to me: "Find out how I can be a better, more trusted leader." He knew the staff had concerns, and he hoped they would be honest and give clear, full feedback to me.

First I asked his team questions they could speak out on, like: What do you love about this leader? What does he do well? What could he improve on? How could the team be more effective? How could he help you do a better job?

The discussion was invigorating and productive as I heard people say things they had held back for a long time. They felt safe and free to be honest, knowing that I would keep names confidential. As the session progressed, I asked private questions, and they gave their answers on note cards, giving them complete anonymity.

As this gutsy team leader paced the halls outside, you could feel the change in the room. The team members, who knew their VP gave both effort and money to bring me to consult with them, had the sense that he was serious about listening to their ideas and criticism. In the future they could talk more easily to him because he took extra care to show that restoring and building trust in their organization was crucial to their success.

Who was the winner here? Every member of the team, including the vice president, was in the winning column that day! The team went on to improve their revenue and results because they had established a sense of trust and loyalty that can only come from the type of vulnerability we experienced in the work session together that day. Taking the time to really listen to feedback reveals care and deepens trust.

### 360° Trust Assessment

One way to get feedback confidentially and foster a climate of trust is by using a 360° Gap Analysis Trust Assessment. Often, when I begin consulting for a group, they admit that they understand the value of trust but have no idea what kind of standing they have with their customers, employees, or community. They want to listen to feedback. They want to know what they do well along with places they may have a weakness. As a remedy to this problem, I've partnered with the leading 360° Gap Analysis expert to provide the Trust Temp 360°, an assessment that improves the trust climate of an organization. It gives individuals and organizations an accurate baseline on their trust. By using it, they can find out not only how trusted they are, but also specific steps they can take to start building trust in the pillars that are weaker. It can be a powerful tool. 360° assessments confidentially and electronically receive information from peers, reports, supervisors, and oneself. People can still tend to avoid them. People who shy away from 360°s need to understand that everyone else already knows where you are strong and weak. Maybe you should know too. A good 360° Gap Analysis is the very best instrument I have found for seeing exactly where one ought to sharpen his or her *Trust Edge*. Visit www.TheTrustEdge.com if you would like to consider whether or not the Trust Temp 360° would be valuable for you or your group.

## "A" Stands for Appreciate

> "The deepest craving of human nature is the need
> to be appreciated." —William James

### Appreciation: The Overlooked Need of Every Person!

One of the tangible ways we show we care is through genuine appreciation. When I speak to a group, I often ask by a show of hands how many feel over-appreciated. Despite putting the question forth hundreds of times to thousands of new faces, I have yet to see a single hand.

---

"Employees' number one complaint is that they are not recognized for their notable performances."[10] —2008 U.S. Department of Labor survey

---

**Ways to Show Appreciation**

- Write a handwritten note.
- Provide peer or public acknowledgment.
- Send a gift basket of chocolate, coffee, or cookies.
- Make a phone call to someone who has gone the extra mile.
- Appreciate people verbally.
- Listen to their needs and expectations.
- Sponsor improvement or valuable training.
- Celebrate accomplishments and good work.
- Offer compassion and flexibility.
- Recognize that work is just part of a person's life.
- Listen to feedback.
- Take action on new decisions. (Not delivering on decisions or promises is a big de-motivator.)

Everyone longs to be appreciated and recognized for his or her hard work and valuable contributions. If you want to change the culture in your organization, one of the most effective things you can do is to catch people doing good work and encourage, appreciate, and thank them for it. If possible acknowledge people in front of peers or in a public setting. People and their accomplishments are what give an organization its value; it is worth getting in the habit of celebrating them.

My long-time friend, Tony, worked many years for a major retailer. He developed a system that saved his company significant time and money—to the tune of tens of thousands of dollars a month. Because of Tony's new system, a process that used to take almost two days could now be done in less than three hours! At the first staff meeting after the successful implementation of this new money-saving system, his manager said nothing but quietly slid a little cardboard package to him. Tony didn't know whether to open it or to remain silent. After getting back to his desk, he discovered that inside the little cardboard box was a standard item used by the company to recognize a job well done. The award paled in comparison to the magnitude of the accomplishment. The award was given in silence —and celebrated by Tony in silence. He told me that he would have rather been given a handshake, a word of appreciation, or a pair of movie tickets. He was never officially acknowledged for his feat, his expertise, nor his diligence. What did Tony do? Feeling underappreciated, he left the company and started his own successful company designing similar systems for other companies. A culture that lacks appreciation is a culture that lacks morale and faces losing talented people.

> **Personalize It**
> Find out the following so you can personalize your method of appreciating people:
> - Their hobbies or interests.
> - How they like to be appreciated.
> - The best recognition they could receive.
> - Who they would most like to be recognized by.

## The Power of the Handwritten Thank You

During my time as area director of K-Life, Inc., I saw the effects of appreciation firsthand. It was a privilege to be a part of an organization while it was growing in size and influence. Certainly many great things beyond me brought about the growth, but one of my secret habits may have made a notable difference. On Friday mornings I took about 20 minutes and wrote appreciation notes. They were sincere, handwritten notes of appreciation for specific things. I wrote them for my staff, my board members, or anyone who had made a difference in our organization over the previous week.

---

**The key to appreciation is sincerity.**

---

An interesting thing happened to me during this process. I developed a heightened awareness of those doing good work around me, as I anticipated this Friday morning routine. In turn, my appreciation spurred more good work. In a short time, the entire attitude and atmosphere around the organization changed. The staff worked harder and with more unity. A new energy and purpose surrounded everything we did. The change was drastic, and it didn't take a new bonus package or incentive structure. My notes were not long or eloquent, but they were heartfelt expressions of gratitude. In this day of instantaneous communication through technology, my handwritten notes were even more meaningful. As I showed appreciation, we experienced a high level of trust in our organization. Together we were gaining *The Trust Edge*.

---

"65% of Americans received no recognition in the workplace last year."[11]

---

### Kindness Spoken Here

Words, and the way we say them, are important. I have a simple reminder up in my office: "Kindness Spoken Here." The way we say things is important, and kind words are powerful. I have also noticed that the words chosen can give much greater impact. For instance, great appreciators focus on the person rather than the object or situation. As an example, it feels good if someone says, "Great party," but it feels *much better* to have someone say, "You are a magnificent host." There is a difference in focus, and there is a difference in how much one feels appreciated.

---

"The number one reason people leave their jobs:
They don't feel appreciated."[12]

---

## "W" Stands for "Wake Up"

"Life is short, stay awake for it!" is the slogan for America's second largest coffee chain, Caribou Coffee. It's also a great slogan for life—even without the caffeine. Life is short. Unfortunately many people go through life in a comatose state, never really engaged with people around them. Several years ago, my wife, Lisa, and I were shopping in the quaint Olympic village at Lake Placid, New York. We went into one of the fanciest shops with $500 Scandinavian sweaters and the latest, most expensive Olympic gear. No one else was around as we looked at and touched the merchandise—not even a cashier. Then I walked by the cash register that was in the center of the store and noticed the cashier on the floor. She was curled up like a cat, asleep on the floor.

While this story is true, it is also true that many people are asleep to opportunities and conversations every day. It is so easy to be focused on the future that we forget to be present with people today. It starts early. Kids can't wait until they are 16 years old and can drive. Then they can't wait until they are 21. Parents look forward to their kids growing up. Employees look forward to the weekend, and to retirement. Soon life is gone, and they were never really present with the people or opportunities that were in front of them each moment.

Just like people are not engaged with people and opportunities, they also lack engagement in their work. I recently read that the estimated amount of time people actually work during their workday is about 40% of the time. What if we could just bring engagement up a little bit by waking up to the moment? What if we could live in the present and show we care? We've all known people who, in the midst of a crowded room, can make you feel like you're the only one that matters. My wife, Lisa, is one of these people. She has the gift of being able to focus and not give in to distractions. She commits herself to the conversation and the person's thoughts and feelings. When you do this, as Lisa does, you demonstrate care and compassion, which works to sharpen your *Trust Edge*.

## "S" Stands for Serve Others Selflessly

### The Trust Agent

When Lisa and I moved to our new house, we knew we were going to add entry steps and a deck, but we didn't want to do it right away. During the home inspection, I learned that I could save money on my homeowner's insurance by adding the stairway to the home's back door. It was evident that we should tackle that project right away, but I didn't have time to do the project myself. My insurance agent volunteered to have his carpenter drive three hours down to our metro area to do the job for me for free. It was a wonderful solution to the problem.

In the years since, I've needed additional policies for my car, real estate, and business. I always return to the same agent because I trust him to do what's best for me. In return, he's retained a great customer, all because he gained my trust by going above and beyond to care for my needs.

The first step in creating stronger connections is learning to think beyond ourselves. In the American mindset, as contrasted to some other cultures, it has become normal to think of ourselves first. We put a priority on looking out for our own goals and well-being. In order to be trusted, however, we need to break free of that mindset. Those who act selflessly give us cause to rely on them. Think of the great leaders who have left a legacy beyond themselves: Martin Luther King Jr., Abraham Lincoln, Jesus, and Mother Teresa. **They were all trusted because they were selfless, sacrificial leaders** who thought beyond their own interests.

---

Only 50% of American workers believe that management is at all concerned with the well-being of their employees. 82% think that senior leadership are helping themselves at the company's expense.[13]

---

## Put People First

In 2001, my wife Lisa and I produced and performed in some large events in Japan. We enjoyed the people, the culture, and the food. Our experience in Japan was a tremendous growth experience, but one incident stood out in my mind as an example of how other cultures are sometimes ahead of us in terms of caring relationships.

We were in a car that belonged to our Japanese producer named Toshi. The American driver backed into a pole that significantly dented Toshi's car's bumper. I will never forget how that Japanese producer reacted. Toshi said, "No problem." In his best English, which was far better than our Japanese, he gave a philosophical treasure: "People important. Car not important. No problem." And with that, the issue was closed.

How much happier could we be if we would only adopt that mindset? How much fuller would our relationships be if we really felt this way? It isn't our cars, computers, televisions, or any other possessions that matter. It's people. Master that principle, and make it a part of your mindset. You'll be more trusted.

---

"If there is any one secret to success, it lies in the ability to get the other person's point of view and see things from that angle as well as your own."—Henry Ford, inventor and American auto icon

---

### You Reap What You Sow

Since 1987, pharmaceutical giant Merck has donated more than 1.8 billion tablets of the generic Ivermectin to combat river blindness disease. The program reaches more than 69 million people, throughout Africa, Latin America, and the Middle East. It began out of a CEO's genuine desire to care for those in need. Not only has their gift saved health and lives, it's turned out to be a public relations windfall, as the contribution, which represents only a small fraction of their yearly profits, pays dividends in the media again and again.[14]

Compare that with the reputation being earned by corporations like State Farm Insurance, who faced a lawsuit from more than 700 Gulf Coast homeowners over State Farm's refusal to honor claims against losses caused by Hurricane Katrina. In the midst of possibly the worst natural disaster in American history, and a personal nightmare for the families living there, the insurer was flayed in the press for their perceived indifference. Showing that your policies are more important than people destroys trust. Companies of all sizes would do well to pay attention to their policies and actions if they are to reflect a value of compassion.[15]

---

The ability to genuinely care for others and think beyond yourself
is a solid—not soft—component of trust.

---

**Care More. Sell More. Enjoy More.**

Top sales people don't just get to where they are because they make a lot of calls, or because they know the best closing techniques. In most cases, their clients have come to see them less as commission earners and more as trusted partners. In those relationships, when the customer recognizes they're truly cared for, they show their satisfaction by buying again and again—and referring you to others.

A good friend of mine and the top sales person for one of the largest A+ mutual insurance companies in America is a very uncommon man. Not only does Scott provide exceptional service and a listening ear, but he also continually gives to his clients. He gives everything from note pads and pens to Harley Davidson Stereos. Every client who buys an insurance product gets flowers immediately. Not only is it his nature to give, but I bet it is hard for another agent to come in and undercut him when they have to peer over the vase of flowers on the counter. When he hears of any client or family of his client being sick, he sends more flowers. He even trusts them to use his condos on the beach. He doesn't use them as a write-off, and he doesn't charge the client. Don't think Scott just became generous once he was successful. Before he had a beachside getaway, he had a heart for service and generosity. He shared one of his mantras with me, "Small deeds are far better than great intentions." Scott considers his role to be a professional servant. He says, "When you serve others and care about them, it all comes back to you." Why does this work? He thinks beyond himself in the most genuine way, treating his clients like friends. As a result, many of them have become friends.

Of course people can *show* compassion for selfish reasons such as recognition or greed. People can "look" concerned when they are not, just like in Academy Award-winning *Slumdog Millionaire*. Two hungry orphan boys, Salim and Jamal, were living in a garbage heap when they were found by Maman, who seemed like a savior at the time. Maman fed the boys and took them to his orphanage with a playground. The boys soon learned that Maman only showed concern in order to own them and teach them how to be beggars on his behalf. But what happened to Maman? He got rich but was angry, stressed, and ultimately murdered by those whom he had taken advantage of. The most powerful compassion is sincere.

## More than Money

In the Western world we often define success in terms of money. Even I have argued how building *The Trust Edge* multiplies profits. I understand the importance of having an eye on the bottom line even if one is passionate about fulfilling a great mission. It often takes money to fulfill the mission. And often the more money, the greater impact and more lasting the legacy. But is success all about money? Is that really the most important legacy we leave? Consider if the success of your leadership, your organization, and your life might be about serving others and the greater humanity. Take a global view. How does what you do affect others? Consider the impact on your closest friends, but also those on the other side of the globe whom you will never meet. Cultivating care for people can be difficult, but the rewards are great. Compassion births trust and adds richness to life, but more importantly it helps you become a conduit for making the world a better place.

## Trusted Teresa

I spoke of the compassion of mothers early in this chapter. Consider the influence of another mother, Mother Teresa. She dedicated her life to caring for the poorest of the poor in the slums of Calcutta, India, and made a greater impact on this world than many of us have dreamed. In 40 countries around the world, over 1 million "co-workers" continue her work of helping the needy. Mother Teresa quietly earned the Nobel Peace Prize in 1979, but her heart was on service. She had something few people knew about. She had deformed feet. Why? Whenever they had a donation of shoes come in, Mother Teresa would search through it and take out the worst pair for herself. She didn't want others to have to wear a pair that was more worn out than what she was wearing. Your goals may be different than Mother Teresa's, but consider her example of compassionate sacrifice.[16]

# Pillar Two: Compassion

¶ Caring leads to trust.

¶ The 4 LAWS of Compassion: Listen, Appreciate, Wake Up, Serve Selflessly.

¶ Sincerity is the key component of appreciation. Consider writing sincere and heartfelt notes of appreciation.

¶ Everybody needs appreciation and recognition.

¶ Put people before things to improve relationships.

¶ Trusted relationships trump clever closing techniques every time.

¶ Care and compassion have bottom-line impact.

¶ Think beyond yourself.

## Ask Yourself ...

1. What could make you a better listener?

   _____

   _____

   _____

2. How could you be more engaged with people in your life?

   _____

   _____

   _____

3. If you reap what you sow, what are you sowing?

   _____

   _____

   _____

4. What do you do to show appreciation to those who work for or with you?

   _____

   _____

   _____

   _____

5. Make a list of five people to whom you would like to write a note of appreciation.

_____

_____

_____

_____

_____

6. The Saratoga Institute survey found that managers believe 89% of employees leave for better pay, but in reality 88% leave for other reasons. Why do you think most people leave their jobs?

_____

_____

_____

_____

7. What kind of sacrifice could you make to show compassion to others?

_____

_____

_____

_____

Without character,
there is no trust.

Without trust,
there are no followers.

Without followers,
leadership
does not exist.

*Chapter Six*

# Pillar Three:
# Character

```
1 1 1 1
```

---

"Nearly all men can stand adversity. If you really want to test a man's character, give him power." —Abraham Lincoln

---

The word "character" is used in so many ways in our culture. If someone has a strong personality, they are described as having a lot of character. If a kid is especially funny, he is a character. If a person is an honest person, she is thought to have good character. Because defining this word is so complex, it is important that we take a close look at the definition as well as explore the two main components of character, integrity, and morality. It is the smart manager who views character as totally relevant to the success of her organization. Let's look at the two main sides of character and then get into some practical ways to gain *The Trust Edge* by nurturing great character.

## The Two Sides

One side of character is integrity. Integrity is being the same in thoughts, words, and actions. One's message and life tell the same story. Hypocrisy kills the message. Had Martin Luther King Jr. preached passivism and yet carried a gun, his message would have been muted. The reason why integrity is only half of the definition of character is because we have people like Adolph Hitler fitting the description of integrity. Hitler had tremendous consistency of character. But most of us would agree that he did not act with high morals.

The second side of character is having high morals by which to live. Even around the globe, most people share a fundamental sense of right and wrong. While it is true that people have differing views on what makes someone a good person, it is not hard to imagine that deceit, arrogance, and selfish ways lead to both career and self-destruction. Those who live according to a strong moral compass enjoy the trust and admiration of those around them, paving the way to success. Moral character often comes from a deep religious or ethical conviction. Without strong morals, a person can think everything is relative, that they personally decide good and bad based on each situation, and that there is no real right and wrong. This type of individual is hard for most to trust. Her decisions are not based on a higher moral code, but rather based on her own judgment. People generally want to trust someone who believes in something beyond themselves. They want to believe in standards based on something strong, logical, and beyond one individual's judgment on a given matter. High morals are hard to teach in an organization, and they are even harder to screen for in an interview. Still, strong ethical leaders can inspire moral character. And by establishing a culture of integrity, those with high morals will be drawn to the organization.

> "Focusing on character changed our company."[1]
> —Tom Hill, President and Chairman of the Board at Kimray

Both integrity and good morals join together to form character, a necessary ingredient for *The Trust Edge*. Like any element of trust, character takes time, intentionality, selflessness, and discipline. We all know that one can get to the top on talent, but only find continued success there because of character. This happens in sports all the time. A great player finds himself a short career because of character deficiencies. In recent years we have seen talented people climb to the top of their companies and even churches and nonprofits, only to see them fall because of a lack of integrity and moral character.

Tony Simmons, Ph.D. of Cornell University's School of Hotel Administration, found a significant link between trusted integrity and profits. He researched staff at 76 hotels using a 1-to-5 scale survey. The study showed an increase of just 1/8 of a point on the issue of Behavioral Integrity can result in the increase of profits by 2.5%. That means a normal hotel increased profits by more than $250,000 per year by having a hotel staff with only slightly higher character. According to Dr. Simmons, organizations that conduct training on integrity maximize profits and earn a lasting competitive advantage.[2]

> "The shortest and surest way to live with honor
> in the world is to be in reality what we would appear to be."
> —Socrates, Greek philosopher (469 BC–399 BC)[3]

PART I
CLARITY
COMPASSION
CHARACTER
COMPETENCY
COMMITMENT
CONNECTION
CONTRIBUTION
CONSISTENCY
PART III
PART IV
PART V

Ben Edwards, the CEO of A.G. Edwards brokerage firm during its glory days, made some interesting comments recently. Though his dad, Presley Edwards, always said, "Hire the smartest people you can," Ben says, "We can hire all the smart young people we want. But these days, we have to look a whole lot harder for character." He went on to talk about how the temptations are so much bigger and the moral ability to handle them seems to have been squelched.[4] High integrity and sound character are hot commodities because they're harder to come by.

Doing what one says is essential to building trust. Great leaders keep their word and take responsibility. They do what is right over what is easy. M.E. Greer, President of the American Society of Safety Engineers, points out, "We can never rise above the limitations of our character," and "If we are going to serve as leaders, then we must have the trust of our followers. Character enables trust to exist and makes being a leader possible."[5] If a person cannot be trusted, who will follow them?

## Milestone's "One Thing"

Founded in 1999, Milestone Systems has quickly become the leading global developer of open platform software for managing IP network-based video surveillance. Certainly they rose to the top quickly because of their unique product that reflects their high competency. In working with Milestone, I have personally been impressed by their industry-setting standards of quality and a culture of innovation. They have created loyal sales partners with 50,000 customers in 90 countries in less than a decade. But one thing impressed me more. Character. Milestone will absolutely NEVER sell around their partners—even if they could make a lot more money selling directly to an end user. Many companies have good intentions, but when they see how they could profit more by selling directly to Walmart or Microsoft, for example, many leave their loyalty behind. Milestone's commitment to sell only to partners and never to the end user has shown that they are committed to their partners and to their word. Their unprecedented success is a direct result of their innovative culture and their sound character.

---

**Advantages of Implementing Character in the Workplace**

- Enhanced morale.
- Increased productivity.
- Reduced staff turnover.
- Improved product/service quality.
- Strengthened customer relationships.
- Lowered workers' compensation.
- Heightened profitability.[6]

---

According to QC Inspection Services Inc., "After only the second year of the character emphasis, [we were] amazed to see a great increase in morale, a decrease of 80% in workers' compensation costs, and a 25% increase in profits, even though the market was depressed. Today, our employees have more than just a job: they are now representatives of a new way of doing business."[7]

---

"The quality of a leader is reflected in the standards they set for themselves."—Ray Kroc, McDonald's founder

---

# Someone's Always Looking (Even if It's Just You)

When I was about 10 years old, my dad and I were out in the bean fields checking the irrigators on our crop farm in North Central Minnesota. We grew semi-truck loads of dark red kidney beans for chili and other foods. On our way from one field to another, my dad swerved the pickup truck over because he saw some trash in the middle of the public dirt road. I knew that I was supposed to "help keep the land clean" so I opened my pickup door and reached down to pick up the trash. It was a *Playboy* magazine. My dad quickly kicked it under the seat of the pickup truck.

We silently drove from field to field and from irrigator to irrigator. I kept thinking about how Dad said that kind of magazine was not the right way to treat women or to have a pure mind, not to mention how it could hurt your wife and marriage. Many times I heard him encourage our tough hired men to grow stronger marriages. I knew that he believed pornography was both damaging and wrong. Yet my dad said nothing about the trash we found.

About midmorning we came into the home area and shop. My dad went to the shop and started working on a tractor. I went into the house to help my mother. A little while later, my mom asked me to get my dad for something. For some reason, I stopped at the small garage door window that looked out toward the shop. I was at least 50 yards from my dad, but I could still see him well. I stood still and watched my dad for a few minutes before going out. There is no way he could see or hear me. And there was no reason he would think I, or anyone, was watching at that moment.

I watched him pull himself out from under the tractor. He opened the door to the blue Chevy pickup truck, reached under the seat, and grabbed the magazine. Then, without glancing down for a single second, he walked with his arm outstretched straight over to our shop stove, where he threw the magazine into the fire.

> Doing the right things when no one is looking
> creates the habits for when people are.

Dad's integrity was challenged that day, but he proved, when nobody was looking, that his character was unshakable. How many fathers, after telling their kids to stay away from such material, would have been tempted to have a quick peek inside? It might seem like a little thing, throwing some trash into the fire, but to me, it was an enormous statement about Dad's character. Most importantly, it was proof that he could be trusted.

> In a 2002 American Management Association survey,
> 1,500 managers were asked what they wanted from their leaders.
> The number one answer, garnering 82% of the responses: Integrity.[8]

## Is This Right?

Character, like Competence and Compassion, doesn't come from going to a seminar or reading a book. While those things can help, character is formed by continued hard work and intentional effort. A great way to get started is by asking the fundamental question: *Am I doing the right thing?*

In every decision in our office, we try to start by asking this question. While most people agree on what is right, the challenge comes in our follow-through to do it. Parents know it would be better to play with their children than to watch television. But it is easier to relax and let the TV entertain. Leaders know it is better to be honest. But it is easier to tell people what they want to hear. People know they should help those in need. But it is easier to stay focused on one's own needs. Doing the right thing takes work! Make the choice. Do what's right.

It can be so easy to tell little white lies because everyone seems to do that in business these days. It can be just as easy to withhold true information from those who have a right to know. Beware. Every decision has consequences. Remember the space shuttle Challenger in 1986? Why did it go up in fire? What was the infamous O-ring failure anyway? It wasn't just a technical failure. It was a collapse of character.

Morton Thiokol (MT), the O-ring manufacturer, was under tremendous pressure to launch on schedule. From what we know now, MT knew the O-rings were a major risk, but rather than take the heat of criticism, they kept silent. Rather than recommend a delay, they agreed with the decision to launch. Standing up for what is right is not easy.[9]

## Learning from Top Businesses and Leaders

Sweden-based companies have topped the list for most trusted businesses in the world for three years straight. Why? One of the reasons may be Swedish Minister of Finance, Anders Borg's stance on doing what is right in spite of pressure to do otherwise. Amidst the economic downturn, Borg drew others together by saying, "[It is] very important to point out that we are trying to solve a crisis and that means doing what is right, not being nice to banks."[10] Thanks to Borg there is a new sense of transparency, responsibility, and trust in Sweden. Others would do well to follow his lead.

An in-flight magazine wrote a profile on the top ten CEOs in America. There were actually no big names on the list. No CEOs with published books or fame for turning the company around. They came from a wide variety of places, backgrounds, and educations. Some were good in the boardroom, and some were not. Some were good on the platform, and some were not. Among the group, there were few similarities but the overriding commonality was integrity!

## We Need Good not Happy

I want desperately to be a man of high integrity. Employees and friends with high integrity are invaluable to me. I want my kids to be congruent too. Have you noticed what you tell your kids when they go out of the house? "Have fun," most parents exclaim. Is that what you really want? I hope they have fun in life, but I never say it. I tell my kids to, "Be good." If the goal is to be happy, they may act in a way that is not good. But if I exhort them to "be good," it generally leads to greater happiness and fewer regrets. Many parents are so worried about their kids' happiness that they don't do what creates good—and ultimately happier kids. Shame and guilt are not entirely bad feelings. I actually want my kids, employees, and friends to feel bad when they do something wrong. People who feel shame for cheating, guilt for lying, and sadness for saying something unkind show that they want to be good. Keep in mind I am not saying that we should guilt or shame people, only that those feelings are a healthy part of our moral compass.[11]

---

A 2007 survey of 1,400 CFOs revealed **integrity** to be the most important quality in a leader.[12] —Robert Half

---

## Whole Foods, Whole Character

In the late 1980s, Whole Foods Company Chairman and CEO, John Mackey, set the pay ceiling for his executives at no more than eight times the pay of an entry-level employee. This ceiling has been raised a few times since then, but Whole Foods Company is one of the few international companies to have a pay ceiling at all. Mackey has successfully opposed the unionization of his stores, not because of a disrespect for his workers, but because his competitive wages and progressive benefits packages would make unionization counter-productive.

Amidst the high growth of the health food store chain, it would have been easy for Mackey to demand a larger salary. Instead, he refused his stock option bonus because it would have violated company rules. Later, Mackey reduced his own salary to $1 per year, donated all his stocks to charity, and set up a $100,000 emergency fund to be used by employees who were facing financial problems. While this was an uncommon gesture for a CEO, Whole Foods employees were not shocked by it. Mackey's character and his priorities were established long before *Fortune* Magazine discovered him.

Mackey set an example for his organization. He's trusted, top to bottom, and has used that trust to spread a vision for greater impact and a stronger company. As a result, Whole Foods has grown from one store to more than 200, becoming the world's largest organic retailer. Profits have grown beyond $200 million. By keeping his word as clean as his food, Mackey's been able to lead his company through an intense period of growth. Though his leadership style is bold and unusual, you cannot argue with his unbelievable level of integrity and resulting success. Mackey has *The Trust Edge*.[13]

## Is Lack of Character a Problem ONLY If...?

Is it only wrong if you get caught? Ask a former presidential candidate. The media broke the story that he had an affair, and a public breach of trust was the result. The senator made a marriage commitment to his wife, and as important, ran his presidential campaign on family values. He deceived his wife, the media, and the country. Now many said, "That is his private life. It has no impact on his leadership." Not true. How can one say that moral character has no impact on public leadership? If one will lie or break private commitments, what makes someone think that person will honor other commitments? He lost trust, and for good reason. Breaking promises is a quick way to lose trust. So is lying, cheating, and trying to sell a Senate seat. Nobody *thinks* they will do these things and yet every day there are new names of those who lost their *Trust Edge* because this pillar crumbled. Choices that maintain our integrity are often made in private. I am all for forgiveness, and I need it as much as anyone. However, we must hold ourselves, our leaders, our teachers, and our politicians to standards of high character if we want to foster positive impact and success in our organizations, our schools, and our government.

## Where it All Starts

We must think about our pattern of thoughts because all actions start as thoughts. The senator did not just suddenly end up in adultery. No way. He had a small thought which led to more thoughts, which created desires, which ultimately led to actions that hurt his leadership, his family, and his sphere of influence. Trusted people control their thoughts because they understand that pure thoughts lead to good actions. Don't underestimate the power of your thoughts. If you are feeding your mind with garbage, whether it be cynicism, selfishness, lust, or a poor attitude, that is what will come out. Good input leads to good output.

"Watch your thoughts, for they become words.
Choose your words, for they become actions.
Understand your actions, for they become habits.
Study your habits, for they will become your character.
Develop your character, for it becomes your destiny."[15]

— John Boe, U.S. Army Captain and author

## Take a Permanent Break from Stress

Many people want to know how to reduce stress. Let me share something that is true in my own life. Procrastination multiplies stress. The number one cause of worrying, stress headaches, and stomach knots is failing to do what needs to be done when it needs to be done. We put off that phone call because we are stressed about it.

This leads to more stress. We put off writing the report because it seems impossible to complete. This leads to more stress. Can you think of something you are putting off? Is it actually creating more stress in your life? I know it is not always easy but, if you commit to meeting your difficult tasks head on, you will have much less stress in your life. From a productivity standpoint, having the character to do the important tasks first is critical.

---

Do what needs to be done, when it needs to be done, whether you feel like it or not.

---

## From a Dingy Apartment to Multimillion-Dollar Momentum

Few firms can say they have too many customers. Even fewer travel agencies are thriving in the current economy because of the new "book-your-travel-online" culture in which we live. Not so for Joe Kimbell, president of World of Travel, Inc. I have had the opportunity to watch Kimbell start selling travel from his post-college basement apartment in the mid 1990s to a multimillion-dollar agency that sends hundreds of groups to the far reaches of the globe every year. How did he do it? Trust.

Kimbell created a clear niche that he is passionate about, group travel. He also sought wisdom from a great mentor. But most importantly, he built long-term relationships by consistently delivering what he promised time and time again. Making personal phone calls, taking time to listen, talk, and follow up, even when things are busy, and quickly responding to inquiries and questions are just what clients have come to expect from Kimbell. Known for high integrity, if

PART I
CLARITY
COMPASSION
CHARACTER
COMPETENCY
COMMITMENT
CONNECTION
CONTRIBUTION
CONSISTENCY
PART III
PART IV
PART V

he ever makes a mistake, he is quick to make it right. If his clients ever make a mistake, he always works hard to make it right for them—frequently at the expense of his own company. For instance, an airline cancelled 18 seats to Russia one week prior to departure. World of Travel had been assured those seats by the airline and his group was counting on them. Needless to say it is hard to find flights a week out for 18 people, but World of Travel did it and ate the costs of thousands of dollars, even though what happened was not their fault. Do you think those clients continue to come back year after year? Absolutely! Kimbell not only builds client relationships, but he also makes friendships based on trust.

Kimbell goes out of his way to make sure his clients have the highest level of confidence in what World of Travel will offer, every time. Kimbell says, "Serving the client, keeping *their* best interests in mind has paid dividends." What kind of dividends? Long-term friendships, more clients than he can handle, and a fun, guilt-free life, knowing he habitually does what is right.[16]

---

Great firms have common thread: good management and high integrity.[17]—Meirine Giggins, Investment Analyst

---

So did Joe Kimbell always have *The Trust Edge*? No. It took time to build. Kimbell served others well. He acted with integrity. He acted consistently and created a clear niche. Kimbell believed in taking the long view in relationships and business. Developing *The Trust Edge* took time. Now Kimbell is enjoying it and all the momentum that goes with it.

> "Not only is ethical behavior in the business world the right
> and principled thing to do, but it has been proven that
> ethical behavior pays off in financial returns."[18]
> —Philippa Foster Black, Director of the Institute of Business Ethics

## Congruent Decisions

I was working with the Better Business Bureau (BBB) of Southern Colorado when I asked the CEO, Carol Odell, what she thought was the key to high character. Keep in mind the BBB's mission is "to be the leader in advancing marketplace trust," which they do through a variety of integrity-promoting programs.[19] Carol said, "Know your values, and make your decisions by them." She is right. For instance, if *respect* is something you value, then making decisions that protect *respect* will be easier. If you have to fire someone, you will do it a certain way because respect is a value. If one values living by the Golden Rule, to treat others as you would like to be treated, then that person will make decisions accordingly. List your top five values to live by. It will make your decision making faster and more congruent.

**Apply It!**

My Personal Values:

1._____

2._____

3._____

4._____

5._____

My wife and I try to be intentional about being congruent in character and in training our kids to have integrity also. We are far from perfect, but one thing that has had an impact, apart from knowing our values and having Personal Mission Statements, is having a Family Mission Statement. Even our two-year-old can recite the Family Mission Statement because we keep it simple and repeat it often. Following the mission statement, we have attached what we call "The 12 Horsager Tenets." The older kids know the tenets. Several years ago Lisa and I were on a date talking about how we could be more intentional with the task of raising our kids. So that evening, we came up with twelve things that we want them to grow up understanding, believing, and living. At most breakfasts in our home, I simply bring one to the forefront of everyone's mind, sharing a little bit of what it means even in the midst of the chaotic mornings at the Horsager household. Of course, the big challenge is that our kids learn more by what they see, than by what they hear. The most important role of the 12 Tenets is to remind Lisa and me to live them every day. To see the 12 Horsager Tenets, go to www. TheTrustEdge.com.

## A QuikTrip to Trust

Named to *Fortune* Magazine's 100 Best Companies to Work For several years in a row, QuikTrip creates a trusted environment by laying a foundation of shared values for over 7,000 employees. The successful convenience store chain, based out of Tulsa, OK, makes a point of getting people behind its unifying value, "Do the right thing for the employee and for the customer." While it might seem simple, this shared value is meaningful and has been a foundation of their notable culture of trust.

One can quickly see how a lack of shared values can kill trust. Consider how the controlling marketing team becomes suspicious of the creative sales team or how the over-working leader has a hard time getting along with the family-oriented employee. Sharing values leads to innovation, freedom, and trust. You have defined your personal values. Now list your team or organization's values as you would like them to be.[20]

**Apply It!**

My Team's Values

1._____

2._____

3._____

4._____

5._____

Once you have values to help define what is right for your organiza tion, the question presented at the beginning of this chapter, "Is this right?" becomes even more powerful. Now the question has defined values to measure against it. If the decision fulfills all of your values, it probably is the right decision. Know your values and make them known. You will enjoy a business climate rich in high character.

## It's Not All About You

If we are going to achieve and enjoy great character, we must consider ALL the stakeholders. Try to go beyond your own interests. Think of the impact of your decisions on the whole family, the whole team, the whole organization, or even the whole world.

## Accountability: How?

Accountability can motivate integrity. While it can be very difficult to create, let's consider a few ideas that have worked:

- Set clearly defined expectations of behavior and outcomes.

- Have the group help create objectives. Co-creation promotes ownership, which increases commitment to follow through.

- Make objectives visible. When expectations are public, things get done.

- Measure results.

- Connect results to consequences. Consider using this idea in conjunction with thoughts from the Compassion Pillar for best results.

- Regularly ask people how they are doing with projects.

- Give appropriate feedback.

- Create buy-in of upper management and ensure that needed resources are available.

---

In an American Management Association poll, 76% of respondents said that ethics and integrity were listed as core values of their company but 32% said their firm's public statements sometimes conflicted with internal messages and realities.[21]

---

## The Problem of Anonymity

A major way to increase accountability is to reduce anonymity. There is a reason that crime is less per capita in small towns; people know each other. They know what each other is up to, and they talk. They know who is at the bar and whose car is parked outside of "that person's" house all night long. While gossip is certainly a negative, small town accountability can promote higher character. If people know they are being watched, they are more likely to act above reproach. This is one of the reasons people do more stupid things in Las Vegas while on a business trip. Anonymity dilutes accountability. This is the reason why some conscientious families move computers into the main living area. By having the computers in a more public space, family members are less likely to go on sites they would be embarrassed to be found searching. And it's the same reason why offices with open work spaces promote greater productivity than ones with solid doors and walls. Colleagues can see whether each other is napping, tweeting, or working.

---

**Five Ways to Build Character**

1. *Be humble.* It is the beginning of wisdom.
2. *Live out your principles and values.* Whether it's "love others," or "do the right thing," living by your principles will make decision making easier and your character more steadfast. Make sure to hire principled people because it is very hard for any of us to learn principles after age 10.

3. *Be intentional.* Integrity does not happen by accident. We are all products of our thoughts and habits. Be intentional about filling your mind with good thoughts. Creating a habit of this internalizes principles and breeds high character.

---

"If you must be a slave to habit, be a slave to good habits."

—Og Mandino, author and sales guru

---

4. *Practice self-discipline.* Being of high character takes the ability to do what is right over what is easy. As Harry S Truman said, "In reading the lives of great men, I found that the first victory they won was over themselves... self-discipline with all of them came first."

5. *Be accountable.* Surround yourself with people who have high expectations for you. Be responsible to yourself first. Lose the pride. Open yourself up to accountability. To see the questions I get asked every week by my accountability partner, go to www.TheTrustEdge.com.

---

"Personal accountability had a 16.5% positive impact on a company's market value."[22]

—Leslie Wilk Braksick, behavior expert and author

---

# Pillar Three: Character

¶ Habits are made by what you do in private.

¶ Integrity builds trust in you—the first step in trusting anyone.

¶ Building integrity takes work, but gives the biggest reward.

¶ Ask yourself: "Is this the right thing?"

¶ To beat stress, do what needs to be done, when it needs to be done, whether you feel like it or not.

¶ Demonstrate character through:
- Humility
- Principles
- Intention
- Self-discipline
- Accountability

## Ask Yourself...

1. Who is someone you admire for high character?

   _____

2. What makes you think of him or her that way?

   _____

   _____

   _____

   _____

3. *Morality* and *integrity* combine to create the Pillar of Character. Why do you think they are both necessary?

   _____

   _____

   _____

   _____

4. If you are the manager, how do you handle an employee who does not show good character?

   _____

   _____

   _____

5. Do you think people in general are more tolerant of low character in certain areas than they used to be? If so, have there been any consequences?

_____

_____

_____

6. What does integrity mean to you?

_____

_____

_____

7. How do you live it out every day?

_____

_____

_____

8. Do you remember your top five personal values?

_____

_____

_____

_____

_____

Humility is the first step to ability.

*Chapter Seven*

# Pillar Four:
# Competency

$$\widehat{\text{1111}}$$

---

"If you think education is expensive, try ignorance." —Benjamin Franklin

---

I love and trust my wife, and yet there are things I don't trust her to do. For instance, I wouldn't count on her to replace the transmission in my car or give me a root canal. I might not trust the mechanic to baby-sit my kids or the dentist with my accounting, but I do trust them to do the job they are competent and capable of doing. Trust is tied to competency and capability. We tend to trust those whom we know can do the job. Captain Chesley Sullenberger, the pilot who safely landed the US Airways jet on the Hudson in January of 2009, is a trusted pilot because of his competency.

Apple Inc. has created a following of committed customers who are willing to pay more than competitors because Apple delivers fresh innovative technology again and again. From iPods, to the Mac Air, to the Mac mini, to iPhones, Apple Inc. has created an environment where high standards of competency result in innovative usable technology. We must be highly competent and increasingly capable in the areas we want to be trusted.

## Google Trust

I mentioned Google in the Clarity chapter, but it is worth noting the story of how the world's most used search engine began. In the fall of 1997, the domain name google.com was registered by two Stanford University students, Larry Page and Sergey Brin. The two men had been working together to improve the way search engines performed. Their idea was not a revolutionary one; public search engines had been in existence for nearly 10 years. What was innovative about their idea was making a good theory more effective, and therefore more accessible, to the general public.

At the time that Google was "born," at least five other companies were also developing search engine technologies with the intention of taking market domination away from Yahoo. If the brainchild of two graduate students was to survive the upcoming techno-battle, it would need to become not only cutting-edge, but also indispensable.

Google first established its competency by simply being an effective search engine. The initial difference between the Google search engine and others was that Google ranked pages based not only on how often a keyword is repeated on the page, but by how often they link to other pages relevant to the particular search. Google was not complacent with just delivering an effective search engine, however.

Google became more convenient to use when they implemented the Google Toolbar in 2000. Now whenever a user is online, they have a very visible and friendly reminder of their favorite search engine. Google has also developed many vertical (more specialized) searches within its search engine. These searches focus on areas such as news articles, book searches, blog searches, academic papers, and videos. Google has since expanded to Google Maps, Google Email, known as Gmail, Google Calendar, Google Analytics (used to analyze website traffic), and Google Earth.

Google's holdings and relevant intellectual property have been expanded through a series of acquisitions. Once acquired by Google, Pyra Labs became Blogger, Upstartle became Google Docs & Spreadsheets, and Earth Viewer became Google Earth. YouTube, JotSpot, and DoubleClick were also absorbed by Google by 2007, along with the technology which created those websites. If it fits with their mission and ups their capability, Google jumps on it and then changes it as necessary to fit their brand.

Google has also been on the cutting edge of web-based advertising—the primary means by which search engines create revenue. In 2000, Google was selling advertisements that would appear on the screen in association with search keywords. Because the ads were keyword linked, cosmetic companies were not paying for advertising aimed at people who were researching car parts. Because the ads were text-based, multiple ads could be placed on the page while the page design remained uncluttered and page loading speed did not suffer.

How long Google can continue to ride the crest of this technological wave must still be seen. What can be determined from Google's short track record, however, is that the company is motivated to stay fresh and innovative in a very fast-moving industry. Google is not yet as large or established as Hewlett-Packard or Microsoft, but the speed with which Google has established its competency was apparent in 2001, when "Google" appeared in *Webster's Dictionary* as a verb, meaning "to use the Google search engine to obtain information about (as a person) on the World Wide Web."[1]

> **Apply It!**
> How can *you* keep learning and innovating to be more competent and capable?
>
> _____
>
> _____
>
> _____

## Competency Drives Trust

In 1979, the "big three" U.S. automakers sold nine out of every ten cars bought in the United States. Currently, they make up less than 40% of domestic purchases, and the erosion is continuing as I write. What happened in the last few decades? Experts and economists say high pension costs, and resistance to new production methods, are two reasons for the collapse of the American auto sector. For most buyers, it came down to competence. Simply put, the Japanese and German automakers produced better automobiles. The collapse of American car manufacturers is all the more stunning when you consider how much of our national pride was tied to the industry. Many families, including mine, considered it their patriotic duty to own and drive domestic cars. But even that wasn't enough to hold off the decline of Ford, GM, and Chrysler. Though people wanted to buy American cars, eventually their collective decline in competency cost them the allegiance of many Americans.[2]

## Learn or Die

> "I don't think much of a man who is not wiser today than he was yesterday." —Abraham Lincoln

According to writer and financial expert, Joe Murtagh, "The world's most admired companies are unable to sustain beating the market for more than 10 to 15 years." In fact, the average life span of today's top companies is less than a decade. Market leaders often fall into a "continued success" mentality that keeps them from learning and succeeding. They lose a sense of urgency and can find it difficult to stay fresh, motivated, and innovative. Bearers of bad news are muted and company systems are set against new ideas. This is exactly what happened in the 1990s when Johnson & Johnson overtook Bayer with Tylenol. Sterling Drug had 50 years of success with Bayer. They knew there was a need for non-aspirin products but would not create something that might compete with their flagship product. They failed to learn and change, and it cost them.[3]

## The Key Competency of our Time

> "Always be in the state of becoming." —Walt Disney

The ability to learn quickly, amidst rapid change and even crisis, is more important than learning any specific skill today. Leadership expert and author Peter Vaill calls it, "Learning as a way of being."[4]

Adjusting, adapting, and learning amidst the chaos of our changing world are certain challenges for today's leaders. A new MBA may feel equipped with many skills, but those specific skills change so quickly in the current environment. The greater need is learning and adapting even in the midst of crisis.

---

Leaders constantly learn and grow. Blamers think they already know.

---

## Farm Growth

No matter what degree we've earned, or what initials come after our nameplate, we *must* keep increasing competency on a daily basis. Growing up on a farm, I learned that healthy things will flourish and sick things will die, whether sheep, corn, or the family dog. It is the same with people and organizations. Healthy ones grow and sick ones become feeble and die. Imagine for a moment that you needed surgery to save your life and had to choose between two doctors to perform it. One stays abreast of the newest procedures, and the other uses outdated equipment and techniques. You would trust the continual learner. Trust is rooted in competency, and you can't achieve that without continuing to learn and grow.

Rick Warren, author of the bestselling *Purpose-Driven Life* and founder and senior pastor of the 22,000-member Saddleback Church in Lake Forest, California, goes so far as to say, "The moment you stop learning, you stop leading." In this attention-span deprived world of mega media and high-tech entertainment, it is critical to carve out the time needed to think, learn, and reflect. Continual learning requires an attitude of sensitivity, humility, openness, and flexibility.

# Keep Learning

I am thankful for the example of my parents who are curious and diligent about continuing to learn. When we asked questions as kids, Mom and Dad directed us to the hardcover set of World Book Encyclopedias. Dad turns 80 this year and has several new hobbies. He learned to windsurf at age 60. When he was 74 years old, he got his pilot's license. Mom continually sews new kinds of quilts and creates new delicacies from her kitchen. Their love for learning about people, cultures, and history is evident. They have traveled the world from the Himalayas of Nepal to the gorge in China to the rivers of Russia to the rugged non-tourist areas of Africa and Australia.

---

"Always keep learning. It keeps you young."

—Patty Berg, U.S. golf legend

---

It's pretty amazing, considering Dad grew up during the Great Depression in North Dakota without electricity or running water. He ran his family farm for a month all by himself in eighth grade while his parents moved things to Minnesota. Mom grew up on a dairy farm where her dad worked hard delivering milk to make enough money. We almost lost our farm a few times due to droughts and falling commodity prices, but Dad and Mom continued to show their willingness and ability to learn and adapt. The farm went from a potato farm to a bean farm to growing alfalfa and later even grass seed for golf courses. Their willingness to diversify, innovate, and be teachable is a big reason for their farming and life success.

## Humility Ability

People trust the humble, not the arrogant. I am consistently amazed at sales people who show a "been-there, done-that" attitude. "Know-it-alls" have a hard time being open to new ideas and better innovation. When I had the opportunity to teach on leadership at one of America's finest military academies, I knew I was speaking to some of our nation's bravest and brightest young men and women. The biggest problem for some of them was that they thought they were too. Though you can hardly blame them for their confidence, the fact is that people do not trust the arrogant. Too much pride turns people off and squelches learning and trust. It also diminishes leadership influence, sales, customer loyalty, and friends. Without humbling yourself to new ideas, you will become stagnant and lose *The Trust Edge*. I am guilty of having strong, stubborn convictions, but I also agree with the old saying that "the mind is like a parachute; it works better when it is open." Is there something you could learn from a person who has a different background, a different way of doing things, or a different communication style? The key to humility is keeping an attitude that there is always more to learn.

---

"If humility speaks of itself, it is gone." —D.L. Moody

---

## Join a Mastermind Group

As humans, we have an amazing capacity to sharpen one another. You see this in teams all the time—a group of motivated people, with a common goal, get more out of themselves than they ever could have alone. It's the power of teamwork, and it is called synergy. Synergy occurs when the output is greater than the sum of

**the parts.** When things work in concert to create an outcome that is more valuable than the total of all individual inputs added together, synergy is manifested.

As professionals, however, we sometimes get so individualistic that we let teamwork fall by the wayside, and we lose the benefits that can come from being a part of a team with a unified purpose. Others might seem like competitors, and we end up trying to fight the world alone. Obviously, this is no path to success. And that's where the support of a mastermind group is helpful.

At the heart of things, a mastermind group is just a term for a group of people who get together to grow collaboratively. I am a part of two groups that fit this idea. One consists of five entrepreneurs from my industry. Once a month, we get together and talk about the issues in front of us. In some cases, we talk over concerns that affect our industry. Other times, we talk about personal challenges. It has become a valuable time for us to discuss our yearly goals, our progress, our struggles, fresh ideas, best practices, and where we'd like to be in the future.

Each one of us, by having a forum to share our ideas and a group to spur us on, has seen dramatic effects in our careers. Some of it has to do with the shared knowledge that shows up in the room. When you're facing a major roadblock, five heads are more likely to have the experience and answers than one.

Accountability encourages us to step up a level and stick with commitments. How many people know exactly what to do, but still don't do it? It might be easy to break promises we make to ourselves. We decide to try something, but then things get difficult and we change our minds. We decide it's not worth it, and since no one knew about our initial resolve, there's no loss—right? Actually, if we lack trust in ourselves, then it is harder for us to trust others.

Within my mastermind group, we make our commitments known. If I say that I'm going to attempt to do something, then I know I'm going to be asked about it at the next meeting. That small bit of accountability keeps me moving forward when it would be easier to quit or stall. The members of my group have really grown to respect and trust one another. We do not dwell on problems, but rather share openly with the goal of helping each other and our respective organizations improve. We have even experienced benefits that we did not expect. I feel as though I'm a better leader, dad, husband, and friend as a result of taking the initiative to start and stick with our group.

There is another four-member group that I have been a part of for 15 years. We are like-minded in our values and commitment to integrity. These deeply trusted friends are free to speak candidly into each others' lives. Besides casual interactions throughout the year, this group meets once a year for a four-day retreat where we share, encourage, challenge, and pray for one another. Even when our group members were living in Louisiana, France, Arkansas, and Oklahoma, we were committed to making this annual event happen. We are better leaders, husbands, fathers, and friends because of it!

Life is better as a team sport. If you really want to get the best out of yourself and make a bigger impact, I strongly recommend you find a circle of like-minded individuals. In some cases, you might start your own. But if you would prefer to join an established group, it's easy to find one for every area and career level. For a list of groups that connect executives or entrepreneurs from non-competing firms in groups of 15 or 20 visit www.TheTrustEdge.com. Being part of a mastermind group is an excellent tool for sharpening your strengths and competencies.

---

"The key to successful living is continuous personal change."

—Robert Quinn, author of *Deep Change*

---

## Read to Learn

My grandmother was known for reading a book a day. I'm not exaggerating! As a matter of fact, she is famous in our family for reading all of the books in two libraries! She had the habit of waking at 4:00 in the morning to have quiet time to read. Grandma Esther loved to learn. Imagine what you could learn just by intentionally reserving time each day to read. I hope to instill this love of reading in my children as well.

Leadership expert John C. Maxwell says, "Not all readers are leaders, but all leaders are readers." One of the outstanding leaders I know is Nate Parks. Whether he is taking his kids to an activity or waiting for the gas tank to fill, he always has a book with him. By having the reading material with him at all times, looking for chances to read a few more pages, Nate reads many books a year. Mrs. Klein, my daughter's kindergarten teacher wisely said, "Reading is critical because in the first three years of school, one learns to read. After that, one reads to learn."

## Seek Nourishment over Fluff

Books are so plentiful in our culture today that we take them for granted. Think for a moment about what you really get when you buy a book. For less than you spend on a restaurant meal, you acquire the author's time, research, and viewpoint on an entire subject. Reading good books gives us a chance to connect with thinkers by investing a bit of our day into seeing things through their eyes. Do that consistently, and you will inherit some of their knowledge and take on fresh ideas and mindsets. Close-minded, selfish people are rarely readers. They feel they don't need to read because their world is all about them and they already feel they know it all. Expand yourself. Step up your reading!

I once took a speed-reading course that was offered at a local college. For a small fee and a handful of evenings, our instructor showed several techniques that allowed me to double my reading speed and increase retention. I'm now able to get through twice as much material in the same amount of time. Even though most of us still read at the same speed we did in middle school, we have the capacity to do much better. I know many people, who with just a little bit of training have quadrupled their reading speed—and as unlikely as it seems, retention almost always increases with speed simply because of focus.

There's a wealth of fresh information in magazines, blogs, and trade journals, and some of that information could make you wiser and more effective in your field. But beware of fluff! Read things that will nourish you, your heart, and your mind. You can find junk almost everywhere, from the middle of a reputable newspaper to an online posting. These petty stories can be the mental equivalent of fast food—it might satisfy our hunger, but it's really just unhealthy filler. So many people start their day by reading fluff that is laced with frivolous stories—some negative and some not even true. Others waste a spectacular amount of time on Facebook, Twitter, or irrelevant blogs. Don't fall for that trap. Give your mind what it really needs, fresh ideas. Think while you read. Pick good material. Expand your thoughts, and you'll gain imagination, fresh ideas, and creativity in return. For a list of reading suggestions go to www.TheTrustEdge.com.

---

> "The man who does not read books has no advantage over the man who can't read them."—Mark Twain

---

## Mentors

---

> "To know the road ahead, ask those coming back."—Chinese Proverb

---

Mentorship has been around since before Socrates mentored Plato who mentored Aristotle who mentored Alexander the Great. The *Merriam Webster's Collegiate Dictionary* defines a mentor as "a trusted counselor or guide." Others might describe a mentor as a wise, loyal, and supportive advisor, or even a coach. Nearly every leader can point to a mentor who played a significant role in his or her success. Guidance I received from experienced men and women has made an enormous difference in my life. Others have seen the issues, made the mistakes, and learned the lessons ahead of you. If you simply take the time to ask them, they're often happy to share what they've learned.

---

> "The key to accomplishment is having a mentor."—Brian Foote

---

PART I

CLARITY

COMPASSION

CHARACTER

COMPETENCY

COMMITMENT

CONNECTION

CONTRIBUTION

CONSISTENCY

PART III

PART IV

PART V

Mentors in the areas of leadership, faith, finances, speaking, and entrepreneurism have played significant roles in my life. Surrounding myself with people who are wiser or more experienced has helped me gain a better perspective on life.

One of my most significant mentoring experiences came during my youth. I was 18 years old and entering the 4-H Youth Development Speech contest for the 10th year in a row. This year would be my last contest. I found out that the winner, out of 2,000 participants statewide, would earn a free trip overseas and would stay with the family of a dignitary. Needless to say, winning the trip was very motivating.

At the county level, I got second place, and thankfully the top two went to districts. At districts, I got second again, the top two going on to the statewide competition. At this point, I knew that to win, I needed to raise my performance to a new level. Over the next five months, I sought help from several speech coaches, a pastor, and one college speech professor. The mentors critiqued and coached me on my speech performance. With their help, expertise, insights, and encouragement, I won the coveted expense-paid trip overseas. I had an unforgettable trip, but more importantly, I learned the value of seeking advice and learning from those more competent than myself.

---

"He who walks with the wise grows wise."[5]

—Solomon, king of Israel (970-928 B.C.)

---

## Individualism or Interdependence?

In America we encourage individualism. We pull ourselves up by our bootstraps and do it alone! Of all the great leaders and influencers in our history, who really did it alone? Nobody. If you want to be a better leader, ask for advice. If you want to be a better parent, spouse, sales person, or golfer, engaging a mentor is the quickest way to improve.

Find someone who is successful in the same way you'd like to be, and just start by asking if you can meet with him or her to ask a few questions. If that leads to an ongoing mentorship, then that is even better. Even in a single meeting, some great mentoring can occur. When I started speaking more, I looked for people who are great on the platform, but also balanced in business, in relationships, and in life. Plenty of good speakers have lost their families, health, and friends. I wanted to find someone who had found a balance.

Former Chairman and CEO of B. Dalton and former CEO of Dayton's Department Stores, Sherm Swenson, was my mentor in college. Sherm chose to spend his retirement working as the Chief Financial Officer for the college I attended, Bethel University. Having made good money during his career and feeling called to serve, Sherm did not work for the pay. I watched as he received big money offers to go back to work as a corporate executive. Each time, he would take a day to think and pray about it, and then politely decline. I watched as he taught his team integrity and leadership. I watched as he laid out big expectations and a grand vision for the university he served. I watched as Sherm skillfully and gracefully dealt with difficult people and difficult situations. I watched and learned. I continue to be grateful for this mentorship opportunity. Sherm Swenson, through conversation and observation, influenced who I became in innumerable ways.

Take the step to be around people who are wise. Be humble. Respect their time. Take seriously their insights. Listen. As my dad, my greatest mentor, often said, "You learn a lot more from listening than you do from talking."

> "Do you wish to rise? Begin by descending.
> You plan a tower that will pierce the clouds?
> Lay first the foundation of humility."
> —St. Augustine, 354-430, Bishop of Hippo

## Be a Mentor

Mentoring made such a difference for me that I now mentor several younger people in entrepreneurism, leadership, and faith. For me, it's not just payback, it's one of the most valuable uses of my time.

Good mentors know how to mix listening and encouragement with candid challenge. It is not thinking you know everything, or that you will fill your mentee with your great knowledge and wisdom. It is about listening, encouraging, sharing experiences that relate, and asking good questions.

# Being a Mentor

| A Mentor Could... | A Mentor Must Not... |
|---|---|
| • Help assess strengths and weaknesses.<br>• Work to develop skills for success.<br>• Demonstrate trust, openness, and honesty.<br>• Work through career and workplace challenges.<br>• Give fresh perspective.<br>• Demonstrate a positive and upbeat outlook.<br>• Facilitate decision-making processes.<br>• Inspire greatness.<br>• Suggest but not force ideas.<br>• Give honest and constructive feedback.<br>• Show neutrality and objectivity.<br>• Help develop self-awareness.<br>• Listen attentively and objectively.<br>• Demonstrate emotional intelligence.<br>• Help with networking. | • Act as a personal counselor.<br>• Bring you to an inappropriate level of dependence.<br>• Do the work you are supposed to do.<br>• Attempt to solve your problems.<br>• Invest in your business or idea(s). |

## Being Mentored

| How to Find a Mentor | A Mentee Should... |
|---|---|
| • Check if your company, church, or organization has a formal mentorship program. <br> • Identify people you respect and admire. <br> • Determine what you need and look for someone with those skills. <br> • Discover their communication style. <br> • Make sure you have shared values. <br> • Find a person you can talk freely with about your career and workplace issues. <br> • Make sure the person isn't intent on changing you to be someone else. <br> • Look for someone regarded as a role model. <br> • Consider people who are trustworthy and can keep information confidential. | • Be honest. <br> • Be open in communicating. <br> • Be trustworthy. <br> • Keep confidences. <br> • Be introspective. <br> • Work under realistic expectations. <br> • Stay accountable. <br> • Admit mistakes and share failures. |

# Tame the TV Time

We are products of what we feed our minds, and it's time for a new diet. In fact, our biggest and most wasteful leisure activity is watching television. It has been linked to an increase in passive behavior, meaning that we become accustomed to watching other people do things, instead of pursuing valuable activities ourselves.

In one study, a manufacturing company examined how much television its workers watched. Their observations were as pointed as they were powerful. The lowest line workers, those assigned to floor assembly, reported that they watched an average of 30 hours per week—more than four hours a day. Moving up the ladder, they found that the supervisors viewed 25 hours each week, still a significant amount, but less than the floor workers. Foremen watched TV an average of 20 hours a week. At a higher level still, plant managers, the men and women in charge of entire factories, reported that they viewed only 15 hours a week. The president watched 8-12 hours per week. Finally, the chairman of the board watched just 2-4 hours a week. Taming the TV time could have a big impact on your career![6]

Further astounding facts about TV-watching:

- The value of the time Americans spend watching TV is estimated at $1.25 trillion per year, assuming a modest wage of $5 per hour.

- 49% of Americans say they watch too much TV.

- Millions of Americans are so hooked on television that they fit the criteria for substance abuse as defined in the official psychiatric manual, according to Rutgers University psychologist Robert Kubey.

- According to Dr. William H. Deitz, of Tufts University School of Medicine, "The easiest way to reduce inactivity is to turn off the TV set. Almost anything else uses more energy than watching TV."[7]

## Daily University

Do you have a daily commute? Do you have a daily workout? What about time spent doing dishes, laundry, or other housework? You could accumulate years of knowledge and expertise by listening to something from which you can learn. Leadership, business, faith, and foreign languages are all great examples of subjects that can, at least to some degree, be mastered through audio courses or podcasts listened to over time. The possibilities are endless.

The key to making this work is *availability*. Have the materials ready (CD, podcast, etc.) by the treadmill or in your car. I love to get on the treadmill in the morning and listen to podcasts or

> **Apply It!**
> 1. Get materials ready for Daily University (podcasts loaded, CDs in the car, etc.)
> 2. Set a specific time for listening.
> 3. Listen and learn.

CDs. I am encouraged, challenged, and freshened for the day. The key for me is preparation. I download the podcasts ahead of time. Decide to learn something new, and start devoting small chunks of time to the cause. Imagine how much you will know in six months or a year if you just start listening and learning a little bit every day.

# Be Intentional with Your Downtime

There has always been something inherently freeing and positive about getting away from the everyday world. Throughout history, great leaders have done their best work by removing themselves from their common distractions.

Beethoven was known for "working while walking," Victor Hugo took afternoons off to refresh, and Alan Greenspan takes daily time to reflect.[8] Sir Isaac Newton worked in his small country cottage for two years. It was during that time away that he began to develop his theories of gravitation and calculus that have made so much of modern science possible. Jesus even got away to pray. Sherm Swenson, my former mentor and the former CEO of B.Dalton Books, took two weeks at a remote house each fall and each spring to refresh. He would get up an hour later than usual, at six instead of five, and take a walk. He said he solved some of his most significant problems during those walks, and so he would always have a small notebook with him. During his time away he would read books, exercise, spend quality downtime with his family during the afternoon hours, and go to bed early. Swenson attributes his effectiveness, freshness, creativity, and longevity as a CEO to those weeks away.

You don't have to be a mathematical genius or a CEO of a large company to need and use downtime. In my own life, nearly all of my sharpest insights and strong decisions have come from a stretch of time away, whether it was taking a solitary walk, spending a week at a quiet lake cabin, or taking a short time to think and reflect at a coffee shop. By being quiet and putting ourselves in a fresh setting, we allow our minds to roam free of the minutia that occupies so much of our daily attention.

PART I

CLARITY

COMPASSION

CHARACTER

COMPETENCY

COMMITMENT

CONNECTION

CONTRIBUTION

CONSISTENCY

PART III

PART IV

PART V

How can we be more intentional with our downtime? Think about a "rest" as it is used in a musical score. A rest is a break in the music and it is very intentional. A rest's purpose is to accentuate and complement the notes around it. Rests are essential for beautiful music, and also for great ideas.

Try to set aside some downtime, whether it be a walk, an extra long shower, an hour in a coffee shop, or a few days at a cabin. Try whatever you can plan for right now. Fresh ideas and renewed energy will help solidify the competency and trust you've gained from those around you. Give yourself space to grow.

# Pillar Four: Competency

¶ Create a regular plan for staying competent and capable.

¶ Humility is the first step in learning.

¶ Stretch your mind with new ideas, fresh thoughts, and different viewpoints.

¶ Find a circle of professionals with whom you can grow and sharpen one another.

¶ Accept accountability in your life.

¶ Find a mentor who is successful or wise in the same way you'd like to be.

¶ Respect your mentor's time and take their insights seriously.

¶ Be intentional about your downtime. Put a priority on creating time to learn and reflect.

## Ask Yourself …

1. Who would you like to be mentored by?

   _____

   _____

2. Who could you mentor?

   _____

   _____

3. Does a mastermind group have a place in your life? If you started one, who might you ask to be in it?

   _____

   _____

4. Who keeps you accountable?

   _____

   _____

5. How do you keep learning?

   _____

   _____

   _____

   _____

   _____

6. Do you, as a leader, enable learning?

_____

_____

7. What can you do to maintain or increase your competency?

_____

_____

_____

_____

8. Would it be valuable for your work group to get away for the sake of rejuvenation, freshness, morale, and innovation?

_____

_____

Sacrifice is the commonality of great leaders.

*Chapter Eight*

# Pillar Five:
# Commitment

---

"Lots of people want to ride with you in the limo,
but what you want is someone who will take the bus with you
when the limo breaks down." —Oprah Winfrey

---

Why were people shocked and amazed when Lee Iacocca
turned around Chrysler but took only a $1 a year salary?
Why did people follow George Washington, Mother Teresa, and
Martin Luther King, Jr.? The causes? Yes. The commitment of each?
Most certainly.

Commitment is what true friends enjoy. There will always be people
who will enjoy your company, laugh at your jokes, and eat your
food, but it's the ones who stick with you when there is effort and
sacrifice involved whom you really trust. This plays itself out again
and again in the business world. When it comes to commitment,

actions definitely speak louder than words. Some colleagues and leaders have demonstrated the tenacity and stubbornness it takes to fulfill a commitment. You know who they are.

In 2009 Caterpillar Inc., the largest supplier of construction equipment, announced executive pay would be cut in half and many salaried employees would see cuts as much as 15%. When executives voluntarily take pay cuts or forfeit bonuses ahead of employee downsizing, the sign of commitment goes a long way in establishing trust.[1]

## A Different Kind of Legacy

In 2008, Richard Fuld, Jr., CEO of Lehman Brothers, said his estimated compensation of $350 million between 2000 and 2007 was appropriate even as he was at the helm of his company heading for disaster at the life-altering expense of many shareholders.[2] According to compensation consultant James Reda, even amidst economic crisis and mismanagement, Merrill Lynch CEO, Stanley O'Neal, exited in 2007 with a package valued at $161 million. Washington Mutual CEO, Kerry Killinger, left with $44 million, and Citigroup CEO, Charles Prince, went home with $105 million in compensation.[3] Former Chairman and CEO of Countrywide Financial, Angelo Mozilo's latest compensation was $132 million despite his company's failings.[4]

---

"67% [of employees] said they were committed to their employers. Only 38% felt their employers were committed to them."[5]

—Del Jones of Gannett News Service

---

Contrast that with the actions of trusted leaders who have left a legacy beyond themselves. Martin Luther King, Jr., for example, endured 30 arrests, physical assaults, and threats against his family, because of his determination that men should live as equals.[6] His commitment to that goal was so obvious to everyone around him, that men and women followed him into angry mobs, trained police dogs, and fire hoses. Would they have stood by his side if they thought he might decide to take the easy way out? Doubtful. It was Martin Luther King Jr.'s conviction that all men should be treated equally that inspired thousands of others to join the struggle. It was this amazing following and partnership that brought civil liberty to a new level.

The strongest leaders in history demonstrated an unwillingness to give in when things were tough, and so they were able to unite others towards their cause. These leaders were committed to something beyond themselves. They were not the kind of people who said, "That's not my problem." Commitment reveals devotion and loyalty.

The executives and managers who succeed today do so partly because they also grasp and embody these traits. Sacrifice for great things. Go out of your way to help others. Show your full commitment to worthy causes and to your team. A sense of commitment solidifies trust.

---

Great leadership demands sacrifice.

---

## Commitment, Harley-Davidson Style

Talk about commitment. One of the most universally popular tattoos is still the shield-and-bars Harley-Davidson logo. The devotion to the

Harley-Davidson brand is unmatched. Harley owners have formed groups, clubs, and gangs for years. Harley Owner's Groups (HOGs) not only ride the motorcycles, but they also wear Harley-Davidson clothes, make annual pilgrimages to the museum in Milwaukee, Wisconsin, or to the playground in Sturgis, South Dakota.

Harley-Davidson was one of only two American motorcycle manufacturers to survive the Great Depression. The company went on to produce 90,000 motorcycles for the U.S. and our Allies during World War II. For many soldiers coming home from the War, Harley-Davidson became a synonym for "motorcycle" and the freewheeling lifestyle that went with it. In the booming postwar economy, the company successfully marketed newer models as recreational machines instead of an Army workhorse. By 1953, with the demise of Indian Motor Company, Harley-Davidson was the only remaining American motorcycle company, but challenges were ahead.

In 1981, a group of American Machinery and Foundry (AMF) executives bought Harley-Davidson from AMF. They took possession of a company that sold overpriced, poorly manufactured motorcycles which were then associated with tattood, rough-looking gang members. What in the world happened? The story is a long one, but the problems they overcame can be summarized into three groups.

- **Problem 1:** The company became complacent with their product, and stagnant technology was the result. This problem was addressed with two solutions. One was the development of the new "evolution" engine. The second was the practice of outsourcing other components (forks, shocks, brakes, etc.) to foreign manufacturers who increased quality and made technical improvements to the components.

- **Problem 2:** Public image was damaged from popular Hollywood biker movies and news reports about the Hell's Angels. This public relations problem was addressed largely through advertising. Rather than attempt to reinvent the company image, Harley-Davidson exploited the "retro" appeal of their motorcycles, building machines that imitated the look and feel of their postwar cycles. This retro image attracted a generation of yuppies who liked to play the part of tough guy on weekends.

- **Problem 3:** The third and largest problem, poor management, required the most innovation and the most time to solve. Japanese motorcycle manufacturers were the competition that nearly destroyed Harley-Davidson. Harley executives had to swallow their pride and adopt some Japanese-style management principles in order to save the company. The notion of quality circles was adopted and extended not only to factory employees, but to dealers as well. Quality circles encouraged real feedback and improvement suggestions.[7]

Had the company not been bought by this adventurous group of executives, it would likely have been liquidated in short order. From an economic perspective, there was no reason to put heroic amounts of time and resources into a company which no longer had a market. This group of executives, however, was not motivated purely by economics. They all had a desire to resurrect an American icon. Fortunately, they also had a very committed group of shop owners and cycle enthusiasts who were motivated by the same goals.

This group of determined, business-savvy motorcycle lovers orchestrated one of the most amazing comebacks in American corporate history. The year 2003 marked the company's 100th year in existence. In order to meet demand for its 100th anniversary models, the company extended its 2003 model year to 14 months. Harley-Davidson now owns 45% of the American heavy motorcycle market. In fact, *USA Today* named Harley-Davidson one of the top 25 stocks to buy over the last 25 years. If you bought stock 25 years ago, you enjoyed a 17,808% increase in your investment.[8]

## Own Up

In my research for this book, I saw time and again how the committed took responsibility for their actions. In our high-litigation culture, there's always someone else to blame. It can be easy to point the finger at suppliers, underlings, partners, and managers that just can't seem to get things right. I have yet to meet this mass of completely incompetent workers, which leads me to think we might be trying to steer some of the fault away from where it belongs—on ourselves. Deflecting blame is no way to build trust. Not only is owning up to our actions the right thing to do, but it can often overcome negative consequences. For an example, we needn't look any farther than former Navy sub commander Scott Waddle, whose ship collided with a Japanese fishing boat, killing nine civilians. Although an investigation determined that some of his men had made errors, Captain Waddle took responsibility for the incident. While he was reprimanded for the accident, he has been largely regarded as a hero for taking full responsibility for his actions and the actions of his crew, never once diverting any criticism to them.[9]

---
Great leaders take responsibility.
---

This lesson is hard for many to learn. Major League Baseball buried itself more deeply under a scandal surrounding the use of illegal steroids. As the media dug in its claws, an interesting trend emerged: The players who have been forthright with their wrongdoings have, by and large, been forgiven. In fact, a few have been praised for their integrity and candor. Imagine that a group of icons, shown to have broken the rules, are vindicated simply by coming clean. On the other hand, some players have been unwavering in their denials, even in the face of overwhelming evidence and testimony. Some may even face criminal and obstruction charges. While everyone has the right to clear his or her name if wrongly accused, being honest in the first place is the right thing to do.

A former neighbor woman continually blamed others for her children's problems, her weight problems, her financial struggles, and her marital issues. She was full of criticism and blame. It is true that all of her struggles were not fully her fault. Very difficult things had happened in her life, but I have never seen a "blamer" succeed until she is willing to take responsibility for the part she can fix. A better strategy for yourself and those you work with is to take personal responsibility and spread praise. Not only will you gain respect, but your organization's climate will inspire a supportive atmosphere where team members are willing to make healthy sacrifices.

## The Extra Mile

I will never forget the words of my mother whenever I was working on a 4-H or homework project. "Go the extra mile. Anyone can do it halfway," she said. My mother was both encouraging and challenging. She was committed to her husband, family, civic groups, church, and our business on the farm. She didn't just say it to me either. She lived it by staying up late into the night to help me go the extra mile. Though I didn't realize it then, she was committed to me learning the value of commitment. It paid off in more than just scholarship money. It gave me a tangible example of commitment and how *The Trust Edge* is earned.

---

Studies have shown that keeping commitments is the quickest way to build trust. Neglecting them is a sure way to destroy trust. Making a commitment to do something for someone else, no matter how trivial it may seem, creates hope in the other party. Keeping that commitment builds trust.[10] —Susan M. Heathfield, human resource expert and author

---

## Under-Promise and Over-Deliver

If you want to build trust and garner the faith and respect of every person in your life, stick to this simple tactic. Consistently do what you say you'll do, when you say you'll do it! Don't even have an answering message that says, "I will get back to you as soon as possible," if you don't really mean it. We have all been misled by leaders, salespeople, politicians, and maybe even friends who have big promises but weak follow-through. Don't be one of them.

When my wife and I had our kitchen totally gutted and remodeled, I paid the contractor too much in advance. They did a super job, until they left, never to return to finish one corner of woodwork and cabinets. We've all worked with people who weren't committed to seeing a project through. Other than it simply being wrong to take the money and leave before your work is done, the contractor simply did not understand the power of keeping his word. Trust and commitment have a direct correlation to long-term profits, solid relationships, and an unwavering reputation.

The graphic design company I work with sure gets this concept. Small, but committed to growing business the right way, Purpose Design consistently delivers more than what is expected, even beyond the contract agreement. In our last project, they promised six designs but delivered 18 superb options! Consistent quality, on time delivery, and attentive customer service has made Purpose Design a treat to work with. They choose clients with discernment and then go above and beyond in order to build trust with their clients. Purpose Design attributes 100% of its growth to word-of-mouth referrals.

## Passion Breeds Commitment

Passion is the essential ingredient for commitment. It's never easy to persevere through hard times, but it's nearly impossible if you aren't passionate about the cause. People who understand what is behind the mission of an organization are more committed and loyal.

Unfortunately, many of them are not thinking past their paycheck, and that's a huge mistake. Money can never replace a burning desire to see a vision to fruition. Most people who have done well financially have done so as a result of doing what they were passionate about. In fact, trying to work only for money is rarely successful. Most of us know of someone who's dabbled in a new career or scheme, because they thought it would put them on the fast track to a bulging bank account. In most cases, they've failed. The promise of a big payday, realistic or not, is simply not enough of a motivator. People crave fulfillment and purpose in their work. Most want to be a part of something that makes an impact beyond them.

## Does Your Company Have a Fan Base?

What do Harley-Davidson and American Girl have in common? They don't just have customers; they have a fan base. American Girl fans resemble Harley-Davidson fans even if American Girl Dolls are mercifully tattoo-free. Once you buy an American Girl doll, you have entered a new world. Doll owners are compelled to buy the clothes, books, and accessories that go with their favorite doll. At their locations in Chicago, Los Angeles, New York, Atlanta, Dallas, and most

**6 Ways to Build a Fan Base**

1. Be unique.
2. Invite customers into a community with the feel of club membership.
3. Communicate often.
4. Give value with every communication (by giving deals, helpful hints, ideas, or furthering the sense of community).
5. Offer more accessories or enhancements that complement the original product.
6. Give fans special treatment.

recently, the Mall of America in Minneapolis, guests can have birthday parties, eat at the restaurant, go shopping, or visit the salon where the dolls can get their hair done or have their ears pierced. It sounds like utter craziness, but if you look past the price tags, you will see that the customers are all buying more than a product. They are buying entrance into a community.

Today, in this individualistic culture, people crave community. If you can create community, commitment and trust will grow. Companies like Harley-Davidson and American Girl have done a masterful job of creating a fan base.

## Blocking, Tackling, and Life

In 2008, Mike Mahlen became the coach with the most wins in Minnesota High School Football history. Bystanders and media alike wondered how he did it since his team is formed by a hodge-podge group of farm kids in one of the smallest conferences in the state. A couple of decades ago, I was one of those kids who had the privilege to see firsthand the power of this committed leader. Coach Mahlen was committed to his players, the team, the community, and to winning. And though he chose to value people over winning, he ran his team as if it were an NFL team. Following long team practices, he spent hours studying film in his office. The results came through, from one Friday to the next, as our small-town team fought its way to win over rivals around the state.

That dedication alone, and the preparedness he brought to his craft every single day, would have impressed anyone. But Coach Mahlen wasn't only committed to football. He didn't just want a team of good players; he wanted to help mold us into strong and good young men.

He really cared about each player as an individual. If you were hurt, he was the first to show up at the doctor's office to make sure you were being cared for. If he saw an issue with character, he would be the first to let you know. If someone was too poor to buy a necessary piece of athletic equipment, he took care of it without embarrassing the kid. Practice was not only a chance to improve our football skills, but also a time to learn some life lessons. Coach Mahlen made sure we all knew that playing the right way was more important than coming away with the biggest score. He saw the best in each player and really believed in them. I doubt I would have become an All-State player under any other coach. Without commitment from the leader, the players will not win. It is the same in every organization.

## Sporting Trust

Many professional sports team fans are extremely committed. They bleed the color of the team, and they wouldn't miss a game. And yet the players, those who actually make up the team, are seldom very committed to the team or the fans. They are committed to themselves.

Every once in a while, we see a glimpse of selfless commitment in the American sports world. Kurt Warner promised that he would give up $1 million a year from his football contract in order to get his friend and teammate, Anquan Boldin, re-signed with his team, the Arizona Cardinals. Warner showed commitment to his friend, his team, his fans, and to winning with his willingness to give up a significant amount of personal salary.[11]

> "Good teams become great ones when the members trust each other enough to surrender the 'me' for the 'we.'"
> —Phil Jackson, Legendary NBA Coach

## Commitment and Courage

There's just something about fighting for what you believe in that makes it possible to stand up, even against insurmountable odds. Social revolutions took place in China in the 1980s when groups of students, fervent in their convictions, decided to risk jail, or worse, to speak out against government positions. In one famous photo, a young man stepped in front of a tank just as it was pulling into Tiananmen Square. Most people have seen a picture or video of that dramatic act. How much money do you think it would have taken to convince him to do that? How much would it take for you? Considering the enormous risk to his life, most of us would pass up the deal at any price. And yet, it happened. Hundreds and thousands of smaller acts just like it take place all the time, not because of money, but because of commitment to a cause.

## One Man's Commitment and Courage

Pat Tillman had already played four seasons with the Arizona Cardinals as a defensive safety when the terrorist attacks of September 11, 2001 occurred. His life is a good example of someone doing what he thought was right, and doing it with commitment and courage. Tillman turned down a three-year, $3.6 million contract with the Arizona Cardinals of the National Football League to enlist in the Army in May of 2002. He enlisted with his younger brother, Kevin.

Tillman said in an interview with NBC News the day after the attacks, "My great grandfather was at Pearl Harbor, and a lot of my family has...gone and fought in wars, and I really haven't done a... thing as far as laying myself on the line like that."

Football friends said Pat Tillman was inspirational both on and off the football field. Both brothers became part of the Rangers, the Army's elite infantry regiment. Pat Tillman was first deployed to Iraq in March 2003 and then sent to Afghanistan. After Tillman's patrol came under fire on a road near Sperah, Afghanistan, about 25 miles southwest of a U.S. base, they got out of their vehicles and gave chase, moving toward the spot of the ambush. Tillman was killed in that firefight.

"Pat knew his purpose in life," said Dave McGinnis, Tillman's former coach with the Cardinals. "He proudly walked away from a career in football to a greater calling."[12]

Pat Tillman will be remembered for his bravery and willingness to sacrifice for what he believed was right.

## Generational Issues and Commitment

The older generation wonders why members of Gen X and Gen Y are not committed and do not work overtime for the sake of the organization. While the younger generation is less committed to the company, I wonder if it is because they have seen how companies are less committed to them. People used to work for decades and retire with benefits after years of service. In today's marketplace we have seen workers lose jobs and pensions dry up just before retirement.

This decline of commitment from corporations presents a bigger problem than many realize. Low commitment means low morale, productivity, focus, and retention.

## Decisions and Actions Reveal Commitment

Recently I consulted and trained at a large hospital on the West Coast. They had very low levels of trust, and it was affecting productivity and attrition. Before flying out to meet with them, I asked about programs they had done in the past. After sharing that they had poured tens of thousands of dollars into training from some of the biggest organizations in the business, I wanted to know what happened. In return for their money, they got some fantastic ideas to make their medical center better, but the problem was that they had not acted on one single bit of the advice. It may be partly the fault of the consultants and trainers, but there was an obvious lack of commitment from hospital leadership to create deep change. Leadership promised to follow up, but never followed through on that commitment. VPs had promised to implement a simple strategy, but failed. This time there was a new CEO, and a readiness for real change was palpable. The commitment to lasting change was obvious and so was the outcome.

# Pillar Five: Commitment

¶ Without commitment from the leader, the players will not win.

¶ The people who stick with you when things are tough are the ones you can really trust.

¶ History's leaders who have made the biggest impact were willing to sacrifice for the greater good.

¶ Passion is the essential ingredient for commitment.

¶ Those committed to worthy causes will go out of their way to help others and make great sacrifices.

¶ A committed organization has fans.

## Ask Yourself

1. How can managers show both trust and loyalty to younger employees?

   _____

   _____

   _____

   _____

2. Are you committed to others? Who?

   _____

   _____

3. For whom or what will you sacrifice?

   _____

   _____

4. Who sacrifices in your company?

   _____

   _____

5. Do you have a supervisor who is committed to your success and growth? Are you?

   _____

   _____

6. Does your company have "fans" who rave about you to others? Who are they?

_____

_____

_____

_____

7. How can you build your organization's fan base?

_____

_____

_____

_____

_____

_____

_____

8. Are you willing to accept full responsibility and spread praise?

_____

_____

_____

Money can never replace
a burning desire
to see a vision
to fruition.

In every interaction
we increase
or decrease trust.

*Chapter Nine*

# Pillar Six:
# Connection

```
 ⌒⌒
 ‖‖‖‖
```

---

I've learned that people will forget what you said, people will forget
what you did, but people will never forget how you made them feel.

—Maya Angelou, American autobiographer and poet

---

At its core, trust is about relationships. It's a way to measure how
we feel about our interactions with the people and organizations
with whom we deal. A study by the Rhode Island based marketing
research firm, MarketingSherpa, found that 86.9% of people
trust a friend's recommendation over a review by
a critic. People like to do business with friends, and friendship
starts with a connection. Increasing connection builds involvement
and engagement.[1]

---

"Trust starts when we show up and engage."

—Dr. Ron Hultgren, CEO, Above the Line Leaders International

---

How can one connect with and engage employees, clients, and stakeholders? American Idol gives you a chance to vote. The Starbucks "I'm in" program pulled in 65,000 people to volunteer over 1.3 million hours of community service. JoinRed.com has engaged companies and customers to buy certain products from companies that are partnering to eliminate AIDS in Africa. Organizations can engage by encouraging input and inviting feedback. Providing opportunities for engagement is especially important for connecting with the younger generations in your organization.

---

Companies that have employees who are engaged in their work increased revenues by 682% and profits by 756% over a 30 year span.[2] —Leslie Wilk Braksick, Ph.D., Chairman of CLG, a premier executive consulting firm

---

## Sir Connection

Great leaders are the ones who inspire a vision and earn trust. They go the extra mile to engage their staff and clients. One leader cut from this cloth is Sir Richard Branson. The fun-loving founder of mega-brand Virgin is well known for his ventures in music, airlines, and mobile phones. A lot of people don't realize that along the way to his $8 billion-a-year empire he's also dabbled in bike rentals, bridal shops, health clubs, and dozens of other markets. Most people, even if they had this kind of money, would find it overwhelming to have their hand in so many diverse markets.

Branson may not understand the intricacies of every business he's involved in, but he understands trust and the importance of connecting with his people. Armed with that wisdom and a sharp eye, he sits at the top of a 350-company pyramid. Branson pulls it off not because he's the sharpest in the boardroom, but because he connects with and inspires others in a way that drives them to succeed. Most of the businesses he starts are run by competent managers who trust him and buy into his vision. On the other side of business, investors who might normally shy away from such a wild array of undertakings overwhelmingly trust Branson. They love and trust his enthusiasm. Richard Branson has earned *The Trust Edge*.[3]

## Caribou and Goliath

On the other side of my city is the headquarters of Caribou Coffee, the country's second-largest java chain to giant Starbucks. Caribou's sales have grown at a compound annual rate of about 22% since 2002. Founded by two newlyweds on a vacation to Alaska, the company has exploded from their Minnesota roots into more than 450 locations across the country. Their brew for success: A personal connection with each customer.[4]

The staff at my Caribou has made a connection with me even though I'm not a daily customer. My standard order is often waiting for me before I have made it to the cashier, and they greet me by name! If I am getting out of my office to write, they know I like to have a glass of water with my coffee. Today, before even setting my briefcase down, one of the baristas brought an ice-cold water to my table.

I have frequented scores of Caribou Coffee shops and I have noticed that this focus on connection is the norm. They know the names of customers. They ask about how people are enjoying their day. They give free refills, free Internet, and a new free drink, if for any reason you don't like the one you ordered. Yesterday, I was at a Caribou and said in amazement to the manager, "It is so busy here. Not a single seat is open." Then I went to the bathroom before ordering, and it was being used. "There really is NO seat available," I joked. They are busy for a reason. They have a culture of connection that promotes loyalty.

At every store, the employees are taught a basic acronym, BAMA: **B**e excellent, not average; **A**ct with urgency; **M**ake a connection; **A**nticipate needs. In fact, finding out about BAMA and what it stood for took no more than a simple question to one employee. Without any hesitation, she explained the policy to me, along with its applications. How many businesses could boast that kind of loyalty, or even competence, from their employees? In many places, especially in food service, this would be just another empty slogan in the company training video. But at Caribou, it's much more than a simple mantra. It stands for a level of connection unmatched by their competition. Caribou does it by keeping their focus on the customer. And because they've earned the loyalty of their customers, the bottom line takes care of itself.

---

"No one can whistle a symphony. It takes an orchestra to play it."
—Halford E. Luccock, 20th century writer and theologian

---

## Finding Common Ground: Questions Build Connection

The accomplished communication and sales trainer Patricia Fripp is right when she says, "The key to connection is conversation. The key to conversation is questions. Therefore learn to ask great questions."[5] It's amazing how much we can learn about our colleagues and friends if we just learn to ask the right questions. When we ask questions we learn about people and have the opportunity to find common ground. When we find something in common, a connection is even more quickly established. If I find out that you have young kids as I do, or if you like riding horses like I do, then it gives us an opportunity to talk deeper about a subject and our connection is strengthened. Yes, celebrate the uniqueness of others. But don't be afraid to enjoy the commonalities.

> "If you really want to be successful in a frontier market, you have to think local, but act global."[6]—Harish Manwani, President, Asia, Africa, Central and Eastern Europe, Unilever

Because we often don't get past the surface, we miss out on a depth of understanding that could allow us to better see the opinions, needs, and challenges of others. This is especially important in sales. I can distinctly remember when this concept began to dawn on me. Early in my career, if you called my office, we would try to convince you how great we were. We would give unsolicited information about our outstanding track record. But over the course of time, we learned to do less and less talking. Now, when a prospective customer reaches us, we spend most of our energy trying to understand their needs, challenges, and desires through asking questions and listening. We seek to listen and talk on the customer's terms knowing they want to find out how our help will benefit them. We ask things like, "What are the challenges in your business?" or "What would be the ideal outcome for your group?" That simple shift in thinking has tremendously increased our new incoming business. By focusing on our client's needs and challenges, rather than spewing out details of our own accomplishments, we put ourselves in a position to help our clients most effectively. If you are a leader, sharing the benefits of the project, rather than making demands creates a feeling of ownership. If you are a teacher, sharing the real-life application creates engagement. Asking questions and then providing solutions forms a solid connection.

---

**Apply It!**

List five good questions you could ask to engage and build connection with a prospective customer or client. Make the questions open ended, meaning they do not have a yes or no answer. They should get at solving the client problems, like: "What keeps you up at night?" "If we succeeded in helping your company, what would be the perfect end result?"

1. _____

2. _____

3. _____

4. _____

5. _____

Now use these questions to increase connection. Ask the questions. Listen. Then provide solutions based on *their* needs.

---

Once you have asked questions, be willing to share a bit about yourself. People want to be known, but they also have a desire to know others, especially their leader. Be willing to appropriately share who you really are.

# Be Magnetic

Magnets are connectors. A magnetic personality is not necessarily extroverted or even charismatic. Some people walk into a room and light it up. Some people quietly draw others toward them by subtle strengths and gentle ways. In either style, magnetic people are more trusted people. We tend to think this ability is innate or special. While certain people do have physical or hereditary traits that draw others in, most of what makes individuals so appealing is a simple set of behaviors and attitudes. One of the most magnetic people I know is an introvert who simply cares about people. People are truly drawn to her. She is a great listener. But she also sees the best in others, avoids complaining, asks engaging questions, and focuses on others. You will not hear her gossip, gripe, or put others down—some of the quickest ways to repel others.

## The Greatest Secret of the Magnetic Person

One secret and irresistible quality of magnetic people is that they're grateful. They are genuinely thankful, and it shows in their interactions with others. Even though we don't usually think of gratefulness as a major personality trait, it actually goes a long way towards shaping who we are. In fact, Dennis Prager, the researcher and talk radio host, conducted a study on happiness for his 1998 book, *Happiness Is a Serious Problem: A Human Nature Repair Manual.* What, he wondered, was the biggest determining factor in happiness? After numerous surveys, he found that the usual suspects—occupation, economic level, relationship status, geographic location, and ethnicity—didn't really matter. Every one of these categories included people who were happy as well as those that were unhappy.

What mattered most? *Gratitude.* People who learn to be thankful are more content and fulfilled. The single greatest commonality of happy people is an attitude of gratitude. And people find that attractive.

Devote a few minutes each day to thinking about what you are thankful for in your life. Some experts recommend making a list of three to five things each morning. It only takes a moment, but many people find that it improves their day and helps them cultivate a habit of gratitude. Become conscious of blessings you take for granted. Does this mean we should not be critical or pessimistic about real injustice? Of course not! But consider the way magnetic traits most often motivate the greatest connection and the greatest good.

| Magnetic Traits | *vs.* | Repellant Traits |
|---|---|---|
| Grateful | *vs.* | Thankless |
| Good listener | *vs.* | Talker only |
| Talks about ideas | *vs.* | Talks about people |
| Sees the positive side | *vs.* | Constantly complaining |
| Optimistic | *vs.* | Pessimistic |
| Encouraging | *vs.* | Critical |
| Honest/Real | *vs.* | Exaggerating |

## Gossip Erodes Trust

While gossip can feel like a good way to connect with someone about a common concern of another person, it really repels. Why? Because if you will gossip about a person not in the room, what is to say that you will not gossip about me when I am not around. For that reason, gossip breeds skepticism and erodes trust. With the presence of gossip, communication becomes guarded and efficiency slows.

## Elevator Speeches are Over-rated

In several fields, but especially sales, the standard advice is that everybody should have an "elevator speech," a succinct 30-second description of what they do and how they can benefit others. The idea behind this notion is you never know who you're going to run into or how much time you're going to have to share.

While it's certainly a good idea to be able to clearly describe your work to new acquaintances, this concept can be a turn-off. We've all been in a social situation and found ourselves next to that person who seems intent on "working the room." Do you really trust people like that? Do you really want to be that person?

---

People want to deal with those who are real and genuine.

---

I'm not suggesting you completely ditch your elevator speech. Instead, I just want to point out it's far more effective to just be real with people. There's no need to turn each sentence into a networking masterpiece. If you really want to make new contacts, get to know them as people. Be kind. Have fun. Hold pleasant conversations. Learn to enjoy people for who they are. Ask questions and listen to what they say. Love people, let them talk, and you'll be a magnet!

## The Greatest Repellant

Stop trivial complaining. It's the kind of fussing that leads you nowhere. This kind of complaining is like a cancer, multiplying the negative feelings in your mind, causing them to fester and grow into more gripes. Give into them often enough and you could turn into a serial whiner. Just as positive attitudes attract positive people, complainers and dissatisfied personalities are often drawn to each other, increasing their collective misery. Complaining also encourages you to avoid taking personal responsibility. It is not positive nor is it solution-centered behavior.

---

Complaining is being negative about something neither party is willing or able to do anything about.

---

My friend Tom, when asked how he is doing, often responds, "I can't complain; it doesn't do any good anyway." Often it really does not do any good. Breaking free of that negative cycle is important. A mentor once challenged me to go 90 days without complaining. My outlook changed almost immediately. A bad attitude is like bad breath—if you have one, people will avoid you, and they probably will not tell you why.

## Exceptions, Exceptions

Of course there are times we must complain. Honesty is healing. Trust is built on being able to express pain and truth without worrying about being judged or devalued. Moreover, there are times we can and should do something about the situation. These are the times we can stand up for justice or for those in need. These are the times we can make something better. We must deal with problems and challenges quickly, transparently, and honestly. To take an issue that we should stand up and do something about and sweep it under the carpet would be lazy and wrong. Call it step one. Stand up and deal with problems and issues boldly. But don't stay in a complaining mode. Move quickly to the next step of finding a solution. Avoid lingering in the problem. And steer clear of complaining when you are unwilling or unable to help the situation.

# Easy Apologies or Genuine Intent

I had a chance to sit down with the CEO of Compass Strategic Investments. For six months, he lived and worked in the Netherlands, so he had some cultural observations to share. One of the distinctions that he noticed was that Americans often make insincere apologies.[7] When it comes to building trust, being able to say we're sorry and doing it sincerely is an important skill. However, insincere apologies, those made out of habit or indifference, are trust killers. Expressing remorse without any real intent to change comes off as insulting or dismissive, like someone who always comes late to a meeting and says, "I'm sorry I'm late." The likely truth is she never really intended to be on time. No one believes her apology, and so she is not trusted.

Do you mean what you say? Whether it is "I am sorry" or, "I will get back to you ASAP," if you can't follow through, don't say it. Make sure you return calls when you say you will and deliver when you say you will. If your intent is good, your words will mean something and you won't have to apologize very often. It's like a mother who says "No" to her child at the candy counter repeatedly with ever increasing volume and intensity. Because the mother has given in to her child's badgering in the past, the child does not trust that Mom means what she says.

The problem also happens when people apologize even though they are not really sorry for what they did. They are only sorry that they got caught. Learning to apologize is only part of it. Doing it sincerely and with genuine intentions is the real test. The next time you feel an apology is in order, ask yourself, *Am I sorry to the degree that I am genuinely going to try to make sure it does not happen again? Do I really mean it?* Of course it is important to apologize, but so is the action that shows you meant it. Those who only need to apologize occasionally, and do it sincerely, will be trusted.

## Be Genuine

When Generation Xers were asked in a survey what their number one question is, they responded, "What is real?" The new generations want to know what is real, what is true, and what is genuine. Why? Perhaps more than any other generation, they have been lied to. From magazine covers with altered bodies and faces, to the invention of reality TV, which is anything but real, Generation X is craving something real. They have watched movies with digitally created humans and have witnessed virtual reality. People today are skeptical for good reason. They hate insincerity. Don't be a fake. People want to know who and what is real and genuine. And if they find it, they trust it.

---

"We've found that our customers want transparency.
They want to know exactly what's going on."[8]
—Bruce Francis, Vice President of Strategy for Salesforce.com

---

## Transparency in Teams = Trust

Another aspect of transparency that builds trust is encouraging appropriate sharing within a team. The better the team members know each other's backgrounds, beliefs, ideals, and other personal aspects, the more likely there is to be empathy and understanding within a group. In groups where people do not have the opportunity to get to know each other personally, questionable behavior is more quickly judged. Assumptions are made rapidly and people feel they are treated unfairly. If teams know your background and intent, then there is a greater willingness to overlook a behavior that would otherwise be judged negatively. Transparency grows trust and, as Patrick Lencioni wrote, "Trust affects how we interpret behavior."[9] Team building, celebrations, off-sites, and social events can be a part of building this transparency that leads to openness, understanding, and trust.

## The Small Business Advantage

96% of people have either "a great deal of trust" or "some trust" in small business. No other private or public institution received this large a vote of confidence.[10] —2007 Harris Interactive poll

Small businesses have a trust-building advantage in today's economic climate. Author and consultant Peter Bregman wrote, "The gap of confidence between small companies and big ones is growing."[11] Why? Big companies have let us down. GM, AIG, and Lehman Brothers used to be hallmarks of security and stability. No longer is that true. Big companies have become symbols of fraud, low accountability, greedy leadership, and mismanagement. Whether you run a Fortune 100 giant or not, you might do well to become like a small company in agility, accountability, and accessibility. Remember that companies are built on good people and good relationships. Connect like a small company and enjoy the benefits.

## Collaborate

Another part of connection is the willingness and ability to collaborate with others inside and outside of your industry. Lose the weights of competition and open yourself up to the possibility of larger influence and impact. In 2009 the Minnesota and Wisconsin governors decided to partner and share services to save taxpayers tens of millions of dollars. No one had done that before. State budgets are supposed to be separate and only for their own taxpayers, right? Not always. Think differently as these two governors did. Think bigger. Be willing to collaborate. So often we try to go it alone out of selfishness, worried about what we might lose by working with others. There is often a greater reward for those who collaborate. A willingness to forge partnerships that show an interest beyond ourselves goes a long way in building trust.

---

"Rebuilding public trust must continue to pre-occupy leaders in both business and public life. Corporate responsibility initiatives and public-private partnerships can play key roles."[12]—Michael Ogrizek, Managing Director and Head of Communications at the World Economic Forum

---

## What's Real in War?

To end this chapter on Connection, I want to share a quote from a friend of mine presently serving in Iraq with our military: "The good news is that the more interaction we have with the locals, the more they tend to trust us. That which is unknown or mysterious or foreign is always easier to manipulate into fear and mistrust."[13]

$$\frown | | | \frown$$

# Pillar Six: Connection

¶ Trust is all about relationships.

¶ Engage your staff.

¶ Ask great questions. Listen.

¶ Care beyond yourself.

¶ Collaborate.

¶ Be genuine.

¶ Be grateful—it is the common trait of the most magnetic people on earth.

¶ Avoid complaining; it repels.

¶ Insincere apologies are trust killers.

## Ask Yourself ...

1. How can you more intentionally connect and collaborate with others?

   _____

   _____

   _____

   _____

2. If you met a prospective client, what would you ask them first?

   _____

   _____

   _____

   _____

3. What are 3-5 things you are happy to have in your life? What are you grateful for?

   _____

   _____

   _____

   _____

   _____

4. What is one magnetic trait that you would like to increase?

_____

_____

5. What one repelling trait would you like to stop?

_____

_____

6. Would you consider the challenge to stop complaining for 90 days?

_____

7. Do you make insincere apologies?

_____

PART I
CLARITY
COMPASSION
CHARACTER
COMPETENCY
COMMITMENT
CONNECTION
CONTRIBUTION
CONSISTENCY
PART III
PART IV
PART V

Doing,
not saying,
builds trust.

*Chapter Ten*

# Pillar Seven:
# Contribution

$$\widehat{1111}$$

---

"However beautiful the strategy, occasionally you should
look at the results." —Winston Churchill

---

## People Trust Results

Contributors deliver results. And results are what make a person indispensable. My friend, Jason Sheard, manages a group of engineers at a product design company. He was one of the first hires at the company a decade ago and has been a part of some extreme growth. Sheard is continually trusted with the highest priority projects. He is an honest communicator who does what he says he will do and delivers results, every time. As with any good leader, it doesn't stop with individual performance. Next to comparable groups, Sheard's team members make twice the profit per person year after year. Being a top contributor is truly a win-win scenario.

Top performers and the colleagues they inspire contribute to the company's bottom line. In return, these individuals are trusted and enjoy tremendous job security.

> "Opportunity is missed by most people because it comes dressed in overalls and looks like work." —Thomas Edison

## Givers

Some people are takers and some people are givers. Takers are only in relationships to receive. Givers invest in others. They offer finances, time, and resources to charities, ministries, and nonprofits. Givers understand the fundamental truth, "The more you give, the more you receive" and "You reap what you sow," but they don't hold their breath waiting to receive. Natural givers are the happiest people I know.

Consider how you can be a giver of:

1. *Attention:* Can you notice or acknowledge people more?
2. *Resources:* Can you set a plan to give away a larger percentage of your income every year? I know a man who gives 90% of his income to impoverished people whom he will never meet.
3. *Time:* Can you spend more time making a positive difference?
4. *Opportunity:* Can you give someone a chance or an opportunity?
5. *Help:* Can you help someone in a practical way?

## Done is Better!

There are plenty of people who want to make a difference, but haven't put their vision into action. Contribution is tied to action. You have to actually do something to get anything done. A friend, author, and small business expert, Mark LeBlanc, says, "Done is better than perfect."[1] What a great statement. We can become paralyzed, because we want something to be perfect. I am all for excellence, but sometimes a line needs to be drawn between finished and perfect. Even as I work on this book project, I think of all the research that I have not shared. There are compelling stories coming out every day that are pertinent to this topic. At some point, good enough and done becomes better than perfect and not done.

Entrepreneurs can have a problem here. They often have a big vision with big ideas. But the reason many new companies fail is a lack of implementation of those

## 6 Ways to Motivate Contribution

1. *Example:* People do what they see. Actions speak much louder than words.

2. *Expectation:* People generally step up to what is expected of them. Expect the best and you just might get it.

3. *Education:* Teach people what they need to know to do their job well.

4. *Encouragement:* No one gets enough of it. Encouragement delivered sincerely is golden.

5. *Empower:* Provide the resources needed to do the job effectively.

6. *Extending Trust:* Done with discernment, extending trust to others proves to be a great motivator of innovation and productivity.

ideas. Two hundred great ideas are worth less than one good idea carried out to completion. The truth is that if people are consistently waiting for you to deliver, you're not only costing them precious hours or days, but you are also destroying their trust in you. Perform great work, but know when to move it to completion.

> The best time to plant a tree is twenty years ago.
> The second best time is today. —Chinese proverb

We will look at some great ideas to be an individual contributor later in the chapter. Before we get to that, let's consider what it takes to be an organization that delivers results:

1. People must be motivated to deliver.
2. Policies must promote getting things done. Too much paper work or too many meetings can hinder results. On the other hand, a lack of accountability for surfing the web or doing personal things is not right and also hampers results.
3. The organization's culture must reward results, but not at the expense of the other Trust Pillars. Recognize people when they deliver results.

## IBM: The Big Contributor

International Business Machines (IBM) has been an unwavering recipient of the business trade journals' annual lists of superlative awards: most admired, most respected, and most trusted, year after year.

Founded in 1911, the company sold everything from commercial scales and industrial time recorders to meat and cheese slicers. Even during the Great Depression, IBM managed to thrive while others went bankrupt. As the U.S. economy plummeted, they decided to produce new equipment. However, the newer and narrower focus was on large custom-built tabulating machines for business customers.

Perhaps the emblem of technological trust began in 1932. A new department was created specifically to lead the engineering, research, and development efforts for the entire IBM product line. The following year, they completed one of the finest modern research and development laboratories in the world in Endicott, New York.

That launched an era of a remarkable line of "firsts" for IBM, including the early stages of computing. They introduced the Mark I, the first machine that could automatically process long numerical computations. The birth of the computer led to IBM's development of FORTRAN, one of the first and most widely used computer languages of the time.

Gaining public trust wasn't an easy accomplishment during the experimental days of computer technology. When IBM announced it would debut the first group of computers to use interchangeable software, *Fortune* magazine called it their "$5 billion gamble." Undeterred, IBM went on to enjoy more successes than failures. Though the company has changed significantly over the years, it still makes history as an industry leader with landmark achievements that are as relevant today as they were then.

IBM's investments in research ultimately produced four Nobel Prize winners, earning them the right to be called one of the most trusted organizations for their contribution to technology.[2]

# Walmart: "Always Low Prices. Always."

Walmart has been criticized for extensive foreign outsourcing, resistance to union representation, and gender discrimination in its stores. Despite all the bad press, Walmart has continued to grow, making it the largest private employer in the world. Six times in the last ten years, Walmart ranked #1 on the Fortune 500 list of America's largest corporations. Its revenues for 2007 were six times that of its nearest U.S. competitor, Target.

So what makes Walmart unstoppable? The company's motto for 19 years explains it all: *Always Low Prices. Always.* And even the Walmart critics will agree that it isn't just an empty slogan. They consistently deliver the lowest prices.

When Sam and Bud Walton were expanding their chain of Ben Franklin variety stores in Arkansas and Missouri, Sam was developing a centralized distribution system. This system would allow him to offer lower markups than his competitors on all the items in his stores. Once Walmart was incorporated and began to spread across the U.S., the Waltons built a network of suppliers who would give them greater wholesale discounts because of their immense volume.

Why do so many other companies live or die by employee morale or public relations blunders, but Walmart seems relatively unscathed? Primarily, because Walmart has earned their customers' trust by making their money go farther.[3]

# Become a Contributor Every Day!

So Walmart and IBM have contributed largely to their industries and to our economy, but how do you improve your individual contribution? Following are some strategies that have changed my effectiveness, and I hope they will help you. Several of them came from spending several days with an incredibly effective leader. I wondered how he could keep such a clean clear desk everyday. I was amazed that he never had more than 10 emails in his inbox except for right when he opened it. I marveled at his peace and ability to get things done without stress or sacrificing time for people. Some of these ideas are simple, but they changed my level of contribution markedly.

---

**10 Key Strategies for Becoming a Daily Contributor**

1. Plan tomorrow today.
2. DMA's (Difference Making Actions)
3. Bundle.
4. Email efficiency.
5. Enjoy a clear desk.
6. Make meetings matter.
7. Make a flight plan.
8. Optimize your computer.
9. Practice the power hour.
10. Decide now.

---

"Never mistake motion for action." —Ernest Hemingway

---

Though an old idea, this is one of the most valuable. It's hard to get a running start on the day without a plan. You don't want to waste your creative morning time wondering what you should do today.

If you want to attack your day instead of having it attack you, use this solid strategy. Take the last 15 minutes of a workday to plan out and prioritize the activities for the next day. This will set you up for success and also keep you from forgetting about important tasks or appointments.

---

"You only live once—but if you work it right, once is enough."
—Joe E. Lewis (1902 – 1971) American comedian and singer

---

Here are a couple strategies to help you out:

- **Run the numbers**. Use this effective strategy to prioritize your To Do List. Count the items on your To Do List, and then number them in order from most important to least important. Use the numbers one through seven, for example, giving the most important item the seven. The next most important item gets a six, and so on.

  After you have finished your first set of numbers, repeat the process, only this time in order of urgency. That is, figure out what must be done soonest and give it a seven, what is second most urgent gets a six, etc. When you are done, add the two numbers together. Those with the highest combined scores are to be done first, and on down through the line. By going through this easy process, you ensure that you're spending your time on what matters most. For some, this may become part of the daily routine. For others, this method may be a one-week learning experience. Give it a try. It will help you prioritize your tasks in a way that makes sense.

*For example:*

| *To-Do Item* | *Importance* | *Urgency* | *Total* |
|---|---|---|---|
| *Finish tax report* | *7* | *7* | *14* |
| *Send demo to Speaker's Bureau* | *4* | *6* | *10* |
| *Write Trust Temp article* | *2* | *4* | *6* |
| *Call Scott* | *6* | *2* | *8* |
| *Approve manuscript* | *3* | *5* | *8* |
| *Update T.T.360 Web header* | *1* | *3* | *4* |
| *Lunch with Joe* | *5* | *1* | *6* |

- **Put it on paper**. Without being overly detailed, write or type your schedule for the day. Documenting your activities will keep you on track toward finishing your work for the day. Crossing finished items off can be very satisfying.

"Every minute you spend planning saves you an average of approximately 10 minutes in execution."[4] —Brian Tracy

DMA stands for *Difference-Making Actions*. DMAs simply give even more focus and intentionality to do the most important things every day by allowing you to only choose five items from your To Do list. This easy strategy has increased our results like nothing else. Make a habit of doing DMAs on a daily basis and your impact will multiply.

**The DMA Strategy:**

1. First thing every morning, take a sticky note.

2. At the top write your most important current goal.

3. Then write the numbers 1-5 down the page.

4. Next to the 1, write the most important thing you could do today to accomplish that goal. Then write the next most important things under 2, 3, 4 and 5.

5. You now have a list of the 5 most important things you could do today that would make the biggest difference in accomplishing your goal and fulfilling your organization's mission.

> Goal: Sell 15 "gadgets" this month.
> 1. Send 5 thank you notes.
> 2. Make 20 sales calls.
> 3. Get feedback from 3 customers: What I could do better? What do they value most?
> 4. Spend 30 minutes researching product attributes.
> 5. Write one article for newsletter.

---

32% of American workers never plan their daily agenda.[5]

---

When you write DMAs, make sure that they are:

- **Focused**. Your DMAs are the most important actions for the day—you shouldn't have any more than five. If you can't boil them down to a few simply stated tasks, then you probably need to narrow your most important goal.

- **Clear and quantifiable**. The focus here is on activities, not outcomes, so know exactly what you are going to do. "Make ten sales calls" or "Spend two hours on the proposal" is much better than "Sell more" or "Work on the proposal."

- **Realistic**. Your DMAs will not be effective if you can't actually do them. Don't write down that you would like to write five proposals in one day when you can only realistically get through two.

Now that you have them, build your day around them. Make sure you prioritize them over all other, meetings, emails, and less important tasks. I hope to have my DMAs accomplished by lunchtime so I complete them before everything else. Then I can respond to other things that come up, but I first did something important that will make a significant impact on my organization and the lives of those we serve.

> Example: *A salesperson who wants to make $10,000 in commission every month might know from experience that he will need to find four new clients. And to find those four new clients, he needs to set one appointment each day, which he should be able to do by making 20 sales calls. He now has a strong DMA: **Make 20 sales calls each morning**. By making this the most important part of his day, he can learn to focus on that goal without being distracted by incoming phone calls, meetings, and other items that are urgent, but less important.*

Suppose you had to prepare a dozen cupcakes. Would you bake them one at a time? Of course not, and yet, that's exactly how some people approach their work. They make a couple of phone calls, write an email, switch back to the phone, then work on a proposal, before they get interrupted by their email again. This kind of activity is counterproductive. It forces your mind to switch gears more often than necessary, and wastes time with each shift.

Luckily, this is one of the easiest tendencies to overcome. All it takes is a willingness to examine your daily workload and decide what tasks would be most efficiently accomplished together.

---

"Efficiency is intelligent laziness."—David Dunham, author

---

Here are a few tips to get you started:

- **Start with the obvious**. Phone calls, emails, and paperwork are prime candidates to be grouped together. In most cases, they can be done more quickly and efficiently in a batch than they can one at a time. You will also want to look through your calendar for other jobs that make sense to group together. Keep an eye toward saving time and staying focused.

- **Set a time limit**. Give yourself a deadline, 30 minutes for example, to finish the grouped jobs. This will keep you focused on getting through them without stalling or procrastinating.

- **Stay in your seat**. When you start working on a group, decide that you will finish them before you get up to do anything else. It will help you concentrate and finish faster.

- **Have a "meeting" day**. If possible, a great way to get through all of your meetings is to bundle them together. Having the meetings back-to-back means it's easier to stay in the right mindset. And, you will have a good reason to keep each one to the point.

---

The cost of interruptions to the U.S. economy
is estimated at $588 billion at year.[6]

---

Email is like a medication. It can cure a lot of things, but there is the potential for some serious side effects. Email can be used as an effective form of communication, or it can be a costly interrupter.

---

"It's not enough to be busy.
The question is: What are we busy about?"

—Henry David Thoreau (1817-1862), philosopher,
abolitionist, naturalist, writer, and poet

---

Before I share how to deal with email every time you use it, get ready to implement the following tips:

- **Close your email**. With your email minimized on your computer screen, you can be interrupted by pop-up notifications and chimes that may occur. That constant interruption takes you away from focusing and being productive. Consider checking all emails that collect in the inbox once in the morning, once at noon, and once late in the day. If your job requires you to be more plugged in than that, check it at the top of every hour. Just make sure it is when you choose, and when several have collected, instead of being interrupted for each one. Taking the first 10 minutes of every hour to check, sort, and respond to emails, will make you much more efficient.

- **Get to 10 or fewer emails in your inbox**. It's easy to get caught up in mounting lists of emails in your Inbox. Two things can happen. First, you spend an exorbitant amount of time reading new emails and sifting through old ones. Secondly, you feel so overwhelmed that you do nothing to address the mountain of email. Important emails could be lost in the abyss. When you have 10 or fewer emails in your Inbox, productivity goes up and it feels great.

To get to 10 or fewer emails in your inbox, take a day to catch up and then do the following whenever you open email. Every message should be handled in one of four ways:

1. *Delete it.* If no follow-up is required, get it out of sight.

2. *File or archive it.* Learn to use the folders, subfolders, and label features in your email system. If you need something for future reference, then you'll be able to pull it up quickly.

3. *Deal with it now.* Sometimes all that's needed is a quick confirmation or other response. If you can answer in two minutes or less, do it right away.

4. *Flag it for follow-up.* If a message needs action, but you aren't ready to deal with it yet, use your program's alert or flag function even if it is just to flag it for tomorrow. The reminder will bring it back to your attention so you can get it out of your Inbox and off of your mind.

---

Your IQ falls 10 points when you're taking constant calls, emails and text messages—the same amount as if you'd lost an entire night's sleep.[7] —University of London study

---

A clear desk leads to a clear mind, which leads to high productivity and laser focus. When you look at your workspace, what do you see? Is it clear and organized, prompting you to begin your most important tasks? Or is it cramped and cluttered, overflowing with printed reports, unopened mail, and an array of sticky notes? The answer might say a lot about how much you get done.

---

"I must create a system, or be enslaved by another man's."

—William Blake (1757 - 1827), English poet

---

Many people have come to think of a disorganized area as the sign of a busy person who is getting lots of things done. Others think the condition of their desk is inevitable based on their personality. While you might lean one way or the other because of your personality, the truth remains. A messy desk invites your mind to wander. No matter what you are doing, your attention is subconsciously pulled this way and that, wondering, *What should I do with that thing?* and *When will I get to those?* Clean desks, on the other hand, lead to productivity and concentration by encouraging you to finish whatever you're working on at the moment.

Regardless of your job or personality, here are some tips to keep your desk free of distractions:

- **One Touch**. Dealing with the same file or piece of mail repeatedly is a waste of time. When something arrives to your desk, decide whether to file it, act on it, or throw it away the first time. Just touch it once.

- **Tickler file**. This idea measurably changed my productivity and effectiveness. A tickler file is where you put paper you need to take action on in the future. To set up this system, clear out one part of a file desk drawer. Put in 12 hanging folders, labeled for each month of the year. Then label manila folders 1-31 to represent the possible days in a month. Put these 31 manila folders inside the current month's hanging folder.

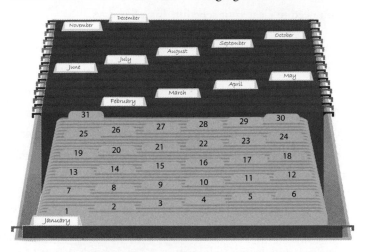

Now, file everything on your desk into the day or month that you want to deal with it. Each day move that day's empty folder to the next month's hanging file. When you get to the end of a month, move that hanging folder to the back of the file, so it can function again in the following year. For example, if it were March 15th, you would have March's hanging folder in the front of your file with manila folder days 15 to 31 in order inside of it. (Days 1-14 would be inside April's hanging folder.) When you get to the office, pull out the manila folder numbered 15 and find exactly what you have to do that day. Then place that folder behind folder number 14 in April.

The great timesaver is this: If I discover a task that doesn't need to be addressed until a later date, then I put it in the day or month I decide I want to see it again. I don't have to think about it or try to remember to do it because it will pop up exactly when I want it to. You get to decide when you want to take action. Another benefit I like is the ability to look at the next few days and re-file or deal with urgent matters—should you need to clear your schedule for a few days.

Build your tickler system in a way that works best for your particular needs. Some people find it simpler to label their manila folders for each week instead of each day which would use just four of them each month. In that case you can just check the folder at the beginning of the week. Some people might find it necessary to have two months of numbered manila day folders.

To keep your desk perfectly clear, you may need to add a few additional hanging files. My extra files include Receipts, Things to Read, and Things to File. Things to File holds papers I file in other filing systems at the end of each month. Things to Read gives me a place to throw magazines and newsletters I can pull out when I know I'll be sitting in the airport with extra time. Think of what additional files you need and create a spot for them. Now, everything on your desk should have a place to be filed. You just need to get in the habit of checking the tickler file each morning.

- **Clean up your office**. Naturally, it's easier to keep your desk clean if your office isn't overflowing with unaddressed paperwork or other distractions. It reminds me of treading water. It's hard enough to tread water when the sea is calm. It's very hard to keep afloat when there are sharks swimming around you. Keep the sharks at bay. Figure out how much time you need each day or each week to maintain a sense of order in your office. You will be able to do your job so much more efficiently.

A messy desk or office isn't the sign of a busy professional; it's the sign of a disorganized one. Make it clear to yourself and others that you want to concentrate and work hard by keeping your space organized for that purpose.

---

Rifling though messy desks wastes 1.5 hours a day.[8] —AOL

---

Long, pointless meetings, a major complaint across every industry, are among the worst in business habits because they kill productivity two ways. They waste time, and they destroy morale. Instead of getting important work done, the staff is packed in a room, listening to a meeting run by someone who didn't prepare. Lack of preparation is an automatic recipe for inefficiency.

It would be silly to suggest we can do away with meetings altogether. After all, it's the synergy created from combining our thoughts and ideas that allows most projects to succeed. But we need to go about them efficiently. Otherwise, they'll drain everyone's time and energy.

---

"The one that claims that it cannot be done should not interrupt the one who is doing it." —Unknown

---

Here are some techniques to make your meetings shorter and more worthwhile:

- **Hold fewer meetings**. Lots of meetings are unnecessary. Eliminate the unproductive ones from your calendar. Perhaps you can be taken off the list because another competent member of your team will be present.

- **Start them off on the right foot**. If you are leading or chairing the meeting, be clear about what you want to accomplish. The clearer your vision or mission for the time, the more likely you are to achieve it. Distributing an agenda in advance will help with the focus of the meeting.

- **Set shorter agendas**. Meetings tend to fill available time. So, if you set aside an hour to go over new initiatives, it's likely to take that long. However, if you make it clear that you expect things to go on for only 15 minutes, there's a much greater chance you will get to the point faster. If the topic can be covered in a short time, 15 minutes or less, consider making it a stand-up meeting. If people sit down, they become very comfortable and become less active in the process of getting through the issues and back to their desks.

- **Schedule them back-to-back**. By having another meeting to go to, you give yourself (and others) a deadline to wrap things up. Use this great method if you have a client or colleague who tends to go on too long. By reminding them of your second appointment, you will force them to be more efficient with your time.

- **Go public**. If you find yourself distracted by office noise or constantly interrupted by staff, try meeting at a coffee shop or other public locale. Make sure your driving time doesn't outweigh the minutes saved.

---

"On an average day, there are 17 million meetings in America."[9]

—Donald Wetmore, President of The Productivity Institute

---

Do you travel for work? These days, getting anywhere takes extra time. Even a domestic flight can take a few hours, and that's without factoring in delays and missed connections. You have a choice to make with that travel time. It can either be lost looking at the seat in front of you, or used doing something productive. Why waste it?

---

"It's the constant and determined effort
that breaks down resistance, sweeps away all obstacles."
—Claude M. Bristo, 1891-1951, American soldier and writer

---

Get the most out of your time by composing a flight plan:

• **Write it down**. Like DMAs, I write my flight plan down on a sticky note. I list the most important things I can do at the airport and during the flight.

• **Come prepared to work**. Make sure to pack any files or documents you will need in a carry-on bag or briefcase. And remember to have the computer battery charged for the flight.

• **Expect the unexpected**. The modern hub and spoke system that airlines use means that more passengers can get more places in the world, most of the time. But it also means that thunderstorms in Zurich can leave you stranded in Kansas City. If you travel much at all, you know that delays are both inevitable and beyond your control. Always bring along something you can work on if you find yourself with an unexpected block of free time.

- **Anticipate your energy level**. An outbound flight to a major conference is a great time to fine-tune your presentation. A return flight of a 10-day trip is not. Recognize that there will be times when you aren't going to be up to doing your best work. You don't have to be productive 100% of the time; just choose your downtime so your downtime doesn't choose you.

Finally, for any travel, ask yourself one question: *How important is this trip?* If your objectives can be accomplished via phone, email, or video conferencing, or if it's more efficient for the other party to come to you, skip the journey altogether. Traveling takes a lot of time, and so does recovering from days away from home and the office. Only take to the skies when you are sure it's necessary. This might require challenging the status quo, but your company will soon learn that you can sometimes accomplish things long distance or with fewer trips.

In 2007, flight delays added up to 170 years of lost time.[10] —*The Washington Post*

## *Daily Contributor Strategy #8*: Optimize Your Computer

How many hours do you spend working on a computer each day? For many it is half or more of your working hours. If too much of that time is spent waiting for your computer to start up and load programs, then you're needlessly wasting time.

Think of your computer a bit like a packhorse. It arrives young, fresh, and quick. But as it ages, and we pile more and more software on its back, it slows down. Eventually, it becomes so overloaded that it moves at a crawl no matter what you ask it to do. It might seem like a minor inconvenience, but consider this: if you spend several minutes each day waiting for your machine to startup and programs to load, you've lost nearly an hour each week.

> "Luck is what happens when preparation meets opportunity."
> —Seneca, Roman Stoic philosopher, statesman, and dramatist

Here are a few ways to cut down on your computer's loading time and increase performance:

- **Ask for help**. If you aren't an expert on computers, find someone who is. Even if your company doesn't have a designated IT department, you probably have a colleague who can help you get things running smoothly.

- **Work on one thing at a time**. Multitasking slows down machines in the same way it does people. Asking your computer to do too many things at once can lead to poor performance, so work on one thing at a time, closing programs and windows as you go.

- **Periodically clean out clutter**. Old emails, file folders, and unused programs are like junk sitting around in your garage. Take some time, part of one Friday afternoon per month for example, and get rid of what you don't need.

- **Do maintenance on downtime**. Most modern computers will run optimization programs themselves, like disk defragmentation, backups, and so on, if you let them. These take time, so set them up to execute automatically overnight or throughout the weekend. It will leave your computer running faster, and won't take up your valuable productive hours.

- **Back everything up**. It is only a matter of time before you will lose something important.

---

The average computer user spends nine minutes every day waiting for files and web screens to download.[11]

---

Writing down your DMAs is one thing, but getting them done is another. Despite our best intentions, we all know how easy it is to get sidetracked and put our most important priorities aside to deal with the most urgent tasks.

In my office, we have a "power hour." It has been a great way to keep at what is most important. It's so simple you might be surprised at how well it works. Take one quiet hour every day.

For 60 minutes each morning, we don't do meetings, phone calls or emails. We don't take any interruptions. Phone calls go to voicemail. Some would say, "You mean you won't take a call from a client to serve them?" My answer is, "No, we won't take a call during that hour so we can serve them even better." Unlike some offices, we can really focus, concentrate, and serve others best by actually getting something done for them. We focus on the activities we identified as most important for long-term impact.

---

"All things are ready, if our minds be so."

—William Shakespeare (1564–1616) English poet and playwright

---

Here's how to make it work for you:

- **Go public.** Let everyone you work with know you are setting aside an hour a day. Informing assistants, customers, and colleagues of your plans means they will be less likely to disturb you.

- **Share the idea**. In my office, everyone gets a quiet hour at the same time. That way, we don't interrupt each other, and we all get more done.

- **Be consistent**. Use the same time every day for your quiet hour, if you can. It will allow those associated with you to get used to your routine, and help reinforce the habit.

Try this method for two weeks, and I guarantee you will be surprised at how much you can accomplish in just 60 minutes. Not only will you make headway on your biggest projects, but you will find that getting your day off to such a strong start will energize you.

---

Constantly distracted workers in busy offices
are able to focus on a task for an average of 11 minutes
before they're interrupted.[12] —University of California study

---

## *Daily Contributor Strategy #10*: Decide Now

The biggest reason we have kitchen counters and desks that are piled high is because we wait to make decisions. We pile our mail on the counter because it doesn't seem urgent. We put stuff on our desk that we plan on getting back to. The non-urgent mail that started out as a neat little pile quickly grows and multiplies into an overwhelming task. Don't let indecision weigh you down. Delayed decision-making causes stress, piles, and wasted time searching for lost items. Avoid huge messes by making little decisions along the way.

---

"Clutter is a result of delayed decisions."

—Audrey Thomas, author and organization expert

---

Decide now and you will give yourself the gift of less stress, greater clarity, and more productivity. Here's how to start:

- **Think**. When you are about to put something down, really think, *Is this where it goes? Am I really going to get back to this? Will I just need to throw this out later?*

- **Take time now**. Write the thank-you note now rather than adding it to your To Do List. Read the report now rather than waiting for the perfect 15-minute break that you never get. Do it, use it, throw it, or complete it, *now*.

---

"Indecision is the thief of opportunity."

—Jim Rohn, 20th-century business philosopher

---

## Lead with Contribution

Contributors not only deliver results personally, but also inspire productivity from their teams. Contributors know how to prioritize in order to get the most important things done first. They don't just talk about it; they do it. They don't waste time, but they don't neglect relationships or activities that build morale either. I have seen some productivity gurus value "productivity" over "people." Those who have *The Trust Edge* find the right balance between people and projects. They get results but not at the expense of relationships. They are givers. No one wants to contribute to a boss who asks for results but doesn't deliver any himself. Be a daily contributor; your example is the best way to inspire a culture of contribution.

# Pillar Seven: Contribution

- ⫿ You must deliver results to be trusted.

- ⫿ The more you give, the more you receive.

- ⫿ Give attention, resources, time, opportunity, and help.

- ⫿ Reward results.

- ⫿ Make sure your Difference-Making Actions are focused, clear and quantifiable, realistic, and consistent with your main vision.

- ⫿ Delayed decision-making increases confusion, clutter, and stress.

## Ask Yourself ...

1.  Do you deliver on promises?

    _____

2.  Do you accomplish results without damaging the other Trust Pillars such as compassion?

    _____

3.  What is a possible DMA for tomorrow?

    _____

    _____

4.  When you think of IBM, what image do you have? Why?

    _____

    _____

5.  How could you be a more significant contributor?

    _____

    _____

6.  What one idea might you implement from the Daily Contributor Ideas?

    _____

    _____

It is the **little** things,
done consistently,
that make the
**biggest** difference.

*Chapter Eleven*

# Pillar Eight:
# Consistency

$$\overbrace{\rule{3cm}{0pt}}^{} \quad 1\,1\,1\,1$$

---

"To be really great in little things, to be truly noble and heroic in
the insipid details of everyday life, is a virtue so rare as to be worthy
of canonization." —Harriet Beecher Stowe, abolitionist and author

---

## Every Time

All of the Pillars are critical, but if they are not practiced
consistently, they crumble. Character once in a while is not
character. Commitment only when you are winning is not commitment. On the other hand, consistent clarity builds a trusted message.
Consistent compassion reveals trusted character. If consistency is
missing, the pillars fall.

McDonald's is trusted because of their consistency. They offer the
exact same burger in Cleveland, Tokyo, and Frankfurt. Really. I
have had one in each place, and they are the same. They deliver the

same product everywhere, everyday. Regardless of whether we love the French fries of the Golden Arches, or protest their nutritional content, we know who they are and what to expect. They give us the same thing every time. Consistency is the only way to build a brand or reputation. A brilliant marketing idea is interesting, but the product is not trusted unless it is consistent. Predictability and reliability are the cornerstones of this pillar. People don't generally like surprises unless a birthday is involved. With consistency comes trust. When we can count on someone to deliver what she says, every single time, she becomes indispensable. What's more, word gets around.

---

The fastest way to build a brand is consistency of message and product.

---

What people say about you matters. It's the reason companies like Amazon encourage reviews, and it's why salespeople need referrals. Those messages carry weight, and they speak to the heart of trust. Earlier in the book, I compared trust to a forest, which takes a lifetime to grow but only a short time to burn. The Pillar of Consistency takes patience to build and must be maintained with care. An instance of broken trust can create doubt, outright suspicion, or even a total loss of relationship.

**Apply It!**

Ask yourself: Am I the same every time? Do I deliver the same quality, act with the same consistency, and speak with the same honesty all of the time regardless of the circumstances or people I am around?

Consistency is like a savings account. Put a little in each day, and over time, it will pay you back in safety and security. Blow it all in one week, you'll be back to square one. There aren't any shortcuts, nor is there a trust lottery. Be faithful in the small things and bigger opportunities will come. You will never get one big chance to be trusted in your life, only millions of small ones.

Consistency of character and performance in spite of circumstances or who is watching is what matters to people. If a football player gives his very best on every down, he will, at some point, make great things happen. Opportunities will open for those who are consistent. To the one who is the same every time, comes influence and trust. Michael Jordan was a mega basketball star because he put on a show every time he took the floor. The actress that creates a following performs solidly over and over in a variety of roles. The leader who delivers a consistent message enjoys a unified team. Consistent customer service results in brand loyalty. To the company that consistently supports creativity and research comes innovation. Consistent marketing promotes gaining market share on the competition. Stop consistent marketing and notice a difference in your bottom line in eight weeks.

---

Only 13% of employees surveyed said that they thought their company had a consistent, systematic approach to business.[1]

---

## FedEx Delivers

FedEx began in 1973 with the simple guarantee of overnight delivery anywhere in the United States. I'm sure sometimes they stumble and miss one, but I have yet to experience it. Because of this strong track record, I trust FedEx. When I send something, I believe in their consistency. Other companies promise the same thing, and some with a lower fee, but people are willing to pay for FedEx, the company that has earned their trust. Under the banner of consistency, FedEx has grown into a global empire, spanning more than 220 countries and handling more than three million packages every day.[2]

---

"This is a guarantee. If we don't get there—we don't get paid."

—Fred Smith, founder of FedEx

---

## Every Interaction Counts

Trust is like oxygen—something that we don't think about all the time, but just like the air we breathe, it plays a vital role in our lives. It's inhaled and exhaled in and out of every relationship we establish and is cleared or clouded by ways we choose to deal with others. Trust increases or decreases with every interaction. This is true for every interaction between a leader and a follower, a sales person and a prospect, a teacher and a student, and a customer and an organization. The leader, salesperson, brand, or product is trusted either more or less based on every single experience.

---

Greater than 75% of employees want an employer
who delivers a consistent message as a top priority.[3]

---

Recently I spoke and stayed with my wife at the beautiful Banff Springs, a castle hotel resort in Banff, Alberta, Canada. When I drove up to the front door I was greeted by name. They took care of my bags and car and assured me that tips were not accepted, but rather these were a part of my stay. They said that it created a more relaxed experience and that people are well paid to deliver great service all of the time. Wow! Great service, meals, and one of the most beautiful views in the world were ours. This resort had captured *The Trust Edge*, until . . .

The next morning, my wife and I enjoyed a buffet at one of the most expensive restaurants at the resort. In contrast to our experience the night before, these servers paid very little attention to us. They did not refill drinks or clear dirty dishes. We watched them talk to each other and care little for their customers. By no means did the poor service ruin our trip, but the trust level in the resort dropped because of their inconsistent service. Every restaurant at the resort was a 10, but that one. Just one inconsistency can change people's perspective.

---

Opportunities will open for those who are consistent.

---

## "Trust Me"

It is action, not words that sharpens *The Trust Edge*. When I recently spoke at a conference for government workers, a public official preceded me. He proudly shared an acronym and told the hundreds of employees that the T stands for Trust. "You need to trust that we are doing this for a reason, and trust that we are doing that for a reason." As I looked out at the audience, I was astonished at the reaction of the people. They clearly did not trust this public official. He lacked sincerity and believability. Just because someone says, "Trust me," that doesn't mean people will. If a sales person whom you just met and hardly know says, "Just trust me," what is your first reaction?

It is not trust! In fact, it is likely suspicion. Trust is not established simply by the words that are used. As a matter of fact, if someone has to ask for your trust, they might not have the ability to earn it. Trust is earned by the actions that are taken.

## Trust vs. Love

True love can be unconditional. Trust is not, nor should it be. I unconditionally love my 6-month-old baby boy, but I don't trust him yet. Trust must be earned. We all know someone who is a lot of fun. We might even have a close friend who is the life of every party. We may love him, but we do not trust him. We enjoy going to the movie with him, but we would never become business partners or leave our children at his house. Trust is the highest value and greatest compliment, and it is reserved for those who earn it. Even where there is love, trust may be broken or weakened. Trust is fragile. A woman can relearn to love someone who has deeply wronged her. However, that does not mean she automatically trusts that person again. The strength of trust depends on the consistency of intent and integrity.

---

"Trust is conditional and fragile."

—Dr. Roger Clarke, principal at Xamax and internationally revered IT consultant

---

## It's All in the Details

Around the turn of the 20th century, one of the world's most prominent doctors was Sir William Osler. A pioneer in diagnosis and treatment, he was known throughout the world. One day, while teaching at the University of Oxford, Dr. Osler announced to his students that he was going to teach them the importance of paying attention to details. For the lesson, he revealed a flask of urine, and informed them that medical science had progressed to the point where the astute doctor could diagnose a patient by tasting the urine. The students gasped. Osler remained serious. He dipped his finger into the flask and then brought a finger to his mouth. He asked his students to do the same.

So respected was Osler that, one by one, his young students followed his instructions, dipping their fingers into the flask and tasting. As the flask made its way from person to person, the young students offered pained expressions, but no complaints, until finally the urine had made its way through the entire group.

Osler resumed his lecture. "If you'd have paid attention," he told them, "you would have noticed that I dipped my middle finger into the urine, but brought my index finger to my mouth. You must learn to pay attention to the details."[4]

## The Best Can Afford to Stay That Way

A Minnesota-based chain of restaurants called Famous Dave's BBQ is known for great food, quick service, and a comfortable atmosphere. Not too long ago, I visited one of their restaurants with my wife and her extended family. We ordered our barbeque ribs and sides, pushed some tables together for our group of 12, and visited while we waited for our food to arrive. We're pretty good at chatting, so quite a bit of time went by before I noticed something odd; people who ordered after us were leaving because they were already done eating.

I made my way up to the cashier, shared my concern, and then sat back down so she could attend to the problem. Almost immediately the manager approached me. He looked like the kind of seasoned veteran you often find in restaurants, 17 or 18 years old with a special shirt and a nametag identifying him as a supervisor. I braced for the worst.

Before I could even speak, the young man sincerely apologized for our wait. He explained that in the rush of business, our order had been misplaced. He quickly retook our order and added free desserts. Not only did he give us our entire food order for free, but he also produced $60 worth of coupons from his pocket, in the hopes that we'd try Famous Dave's BBQ again on another occasion soon.

Do you think we love and trust Famous Dave's? Of course we do! But the point I'm making is about more than Famous Dave's stellar customer service. It is about the fact that they could *afford* to handle the misplaced food order in that way. Most companies would be out of business in short order if they had to go that far in fixing their own gaffes. But Famous Dave's is so consistent in offering delicious food, a great atmosphere, and a reason to be trusted that they can afford to turn the few mistakes they make into positive experiences for their customers.

## What Makes the Biggest Difference?

Many people mistakenly focus on the BIG things. Leadership guru James Garlow wrote, "If you don't like who you have become, it is because of the thousands of small, seemingly insignificant decisions that you have made each day over the course of the years. If you like what you have become and are becoming, it is because you have made several hundred thousand seemingly small, moment-by-moment decisions in a very wise manner. You are the sum total of your life's decisions."[5]

---

"Success is the sum of details."—Harry Firestone, Founder of the Firestone Tire and Rubber Company

---

There are some circumstances beyond our control, but for the most part, we are the result of our collective actions and decisions. If a man is overweight, it's because he's eaten too many calories for a long time, not because he had a big dinner the night before. If a man is a good husband, it's not because he brought his wife flowers and chocolates yesterday, but rather, because he's been faithful and caring to her over many years. If a woman is a great manager, it is because she is frequently sharing her vision, encouraging her team, and aligning others with her vision. While it is worth celebrating BIG things, it is the little things done consistently, that sharpen *The Trust Edge*.

---

**Apply It!**

None of these will change your life much if you do it once. However, do just one of these suggestions consistently over time and see dramatic change.

❑ Take the stairs instead of the elevator.

❑ Eat healthy food.

❑ Read good books.

❑ Find a mentor/be a mentor.

❑ Write in a journal.

---

- ❑ Plan get-away time.
- ❑ Drink water instead of soda.
- ❑ Volunteer.
- ❑ Pray.
- ❑ Exercise.
- ❑ Cut TV time.
- ❑ Be around great people and emulate them.
- ❑ Write thank-you notes.
- ❑ Listen to good music or messages.
- ❑ Take time to think and dream.
- ❑ Go out on a date with your significant other.
- ❑ Be grateful.

Write down one little thing that, if you do it consistently for the next 90 days, will change your life for the better in your:

Work:_____

_____

Relationships:_____

_____

Health:_____

_____

Family life: _____

_____

Finances: _____

_____

# Consistency Builds Habits

Changing habits is not easy. However, it can be very worth it. You may have experienced either of the two major pains in life: the pain of discipline or the pain of regret. The pain of discipline is better!

---

"We are what we repeatedly do.
Excellence, then, is not an act, but a habit."

—Aristotle, ancient Greek philosopher, scientist, and physician

---

Habits don't change on their own, and even with good intentions, they are difficult to alter. If we are serious about changing a habit, it is necessary to take the steps that will create an environment where we can succeed. I can remember when I basically stopped watching TV and the difference that made in my life. I have a friend who lost 85 pounds over the last six months by following some of the subsequent steps that help create a habit-changing environment:

1. *Write down the habit* you want to change. Writing it down solidifies commitment.

2. *Note the benefits* of changing and consequences of not changing.

3. *Replace it.* It is easier to "replace" a habit than to "quit" it. For instance, replace watching TV with playing racquetball or reading rather than simply stopping the tube addiction.

4. *Work on one habit at a time.*

5. *Create a clear plan.*

6. *Break the plan down* into daily actions.

7. *Create appropriate accountability* through a trusted friend or professional.

8. *Reward* the target behavior.

9. *Keep it on top of your mind* (post-its or phone/email reminders can help).

10. *Remove distractions.*

11. *Ask for help.*

---

"First we make our habits, then our habits make us."

—Charles C. Noble

---

# Pillar Eight: Consistency

⊓ Consistency leads to trust.

⊓ Deliver the same every time, and you will become trusted.

⊓ The track record of trust is built over time. There is no other way to lasting success.

⊓ Don't agree to anything you can't deliver.

⊓ You increase or decrease trust with every interaction.

⊓ Trust is earned by consistent action not just words.

## Ask Yourself ...

1. Are you consistent in words and actions?

   _____

2. How could you be more consistent in your
   communications?

   _____

   _____

3. How could your organization be more
   consistent?

   _____

   _____

   _____

4. What one thing, if you did it consistently over
   the next 6 months, would change your life?

   _____

   _____

5. Can you think of an inconsistent retail experience and how it made you feel? Will you go
   back?

   _____

   _____

   _____

# PART III
## TRANSFORMING TRUST

Transforming trust is the kind that truly changes a relationship. Extending the right amount of trust to others changes a relationship because it gives a person the opportunity to be her best. Rebuilding trust changes a relationship even more drastically. Sometimes people can hardly imagine that trust could be rebuilt. The truth is, trust can be rebuilt stronger than ever before.

It is not so bad
to be lied to.

The bigger problem
is my loss of ability
to believe in you.

# Chapter Twelve

# Extending Trust

## 1111

"Few things can help an individual more than to
place responsibility on him, and to let him know that you trust him."
—Booker T. Washington, 1856-1915 author, and Civil Rights leader

B ecoming trustworthy ourselves, although not easy, is far less
complex than the concept of extending trust to others. Practicing
the 8 Pillars to build trust takes personal fortitude and patience.
However, in that case, the personal change required depends only
on you, whereas the result of extending trust to others depends on a
myriad of outside sources and unknowns. Given the unknowns, we
wade into the waters of extending trust with caution. As we will see,
there are pearls to be found. Trust does hold its value, even amidst
unpredictability.

# Intelligent Risk = Big Rewards

It can be safely assumed that loaning money to complete strangers involves a significant risk. After all, how do you know if they would pay it back? So lending money in the developing world, across language and cultural barriers, to the working poor, would be much too risky, right? Wrong. This is the business model behind Opportunity International, one of the first nonprofit organizations to recognize the benefits of providing small business loans as capital to those working their way out of poverty. A resounding success, Opportunity is a shining example of what happens when trust is extended.

Founded in 1971 by Al Whittaker, former president of Bristol Myers International Corporation in America, and Australian entrepreneur David Bussau, the organization now provides financial services to more than two million clients in over 20 countries in the developing world. Their community banking model allows the organization to leverage donations with commercial borrowings and its clients' own savings to significantly increase the size of its loan pool and provide additional funds for its work. Over the last five years, Opportunity International has received approximately $350 million in donations and loaned out nearly $3 billion, resulting in 8.8 million small business loans.

How does Opportunity work? Ten to 30 entrepreneurs, mostly women, join together as a Trust Group to guarantee each other's loans and support one another. If one member is not able to pay their portion of the loan one month, the others must chip in to make that person's payment to keep all loans current for the entire Trust Group. Because the group guarantee replaces the need for collateral, loans become possible for the poorest of the poor—even those living in garbage dumps who have previously been excluded from such financial services.

Through their involvement with Opportunity International, each entrepreneur is highly motivated to succeed. Opportunity supports each Trust Group through financial training and peer participation. Donors who are introduced to the organization are moved by the mission, compelled by its historic 98% payback rate, engaged by the personal success stories, and intrigued by the organization's transparency.

Opportunity International has done what appeared to be an impossible task at first glance. They have empowered the poor in Third World nations to *lift themselves* out of poverty. By thoughtfully extending trust to groups of women entrepreneurs who are dedicated to the welfare of their families, Opportunity has positively impacted individuals, families, and communities across the globe.[1]

## Benefits of Extending Trust: Motivation

Most often the greater the risk, the greater the reward. When extending trust to a person, your expectations of them meld together with your belief in them, which inspires success. Many people believed in me so strongly through my youth that I truly believed in myself as a result. What is expected of a person will likely be what they aspire to. If a person senses low expectations, she will aim low. If a person senses high expectations as well as support and trust, she will aim high and most likely use more of her potential.

My wife, Lisa, said something profound at her grandmother's funeral. "My grandma believed in me no matter what. I was always the smartest, most beautiful, most wonderful in her eyes. You have got to have someone who believes in you like that, even if they are wrong—especially if they are wrong!" Lisa is right.

PART I

CLARITY

COMPASSION

CHARACTER

COMPETENCY

COMMITMENT

CONNECTION

CONTRIBUTION

CONSISTENCY

PART III

PART IV

PART V

People, employees, and leaders all need someone to believe in them. It brings out the best. It reminds me of Coach Mahlen, whom I mentioned earlier. We almost always won in football, in large part because Coach Mahlen believed in us. Believe in those around you, and let them know you believe in them. The rewards of extending trust can be truly extraordinary. Do it. You just might have a front row seat to something special.

## Barkley Believes

Anyone who has worked as a waiter or waitress can understand that waiting tables can be a test of trust in the generosity of others. A table-section can be seen as a small business of sorts, with the waiter as entrepreneur. When one's entire "paycheck" is derived from implicit contracts called "tips," it is a relationship built on trust. One trusts that good food and drinks will be provided in a timely, pleasant manner. The other trusts a fair tip will be coming for the service provided.

Charles Barkley, the former NBA basketball star, changed that experience for one young waiter, Christian Abate, and it is a multi-faceted example of the power of extending trust.

Abate was a young student who was studying to become a teacher at Temple University. Due to financial hardships, however, he dropped out of college to work as a waiter. When Charles Barkley heard this story, he was disappointed beyond words. After some thought, Barkley gave this young man a college-tuition sized tip. In extending trust, one just does not know what will happen. But the risk is often worth it. In this case, Abate handled the large gift responsibly. He is now a trusted teacher to many Philadelphia children. By extending trust, Charles Barkley added value to not only one man, but also to a host of other students and families he will never even know.[2]

I have worked for boards and leaders who trusted me to do a great job, but I have also worked for controlling micro-managers. Trust motivated me to do my best, and I have noticed that it gets the best out of nearly everyone. Expectations and trust motivate teams to sacrifice and meet great challenges.

You can get more from people by believing in them and letting them know they have your confidence. Trust is a great motivator. Try letting go and saying the following phrases sincerely more often:

- "I know you can do it."
- "I am glad you are on this project. You always make great contributions."
- "I believe in you. Let me know if I can do anything to help."
- "I have confidence in you and your decisions. Let me know if you need any resources."

## Extend Trust to Gain Efficiency and Effectiveness

I once worked for a man who was very talented and accomplished, but had trouble trusting his staff. The atmosphere around his office was tense, and nobody wanted to be the one to make a mistake that would draw his ire. We felt no freedom to act creatively, and the threat of failing to meet his demands was a constant. As a result, productivity decreased and morale tanked. This is what happens when there are great expectations, but no trust. People crumble in this environment. Where there is a lack of trust, everything costs more, takes more time, and creates more hassles. Extending trust inspires greater efficiency and effectiveness.

Robert K. Cooper and Ayman Sawarf's story in *Executive EQ* is a beautiful example of extending trust in action. Read on and see how the former CEO of Southwest Airlines Herb Kelleher benefits in time and effort because he is able to quickly extend trust to his leadership team.

> One day, Gary Barron, executive vice-president at Southwest, caught Kelleher in a hallway after a meeting. Barron told Kelleher he wanted to talk about the complete reorganization of the management structure of Southwest's $700 million maintenance department. He handed Kelleher a three-page summary of the plan. The CEO read it on the spot, and raised only one concern. Barron said that it was something he was concerned about too, and was dealing with it. "Then it is fine by me," replied Kelleher. "Go ahead." The entire conversation took about four minutes. Kelleher is respected and has credibility with his employees.[3]

---

Don't tell people how to do things, tell them what to do and let them surprise you with their results."

—General George Patton

---

## Snowball Effect

When a trusting environment is created, the value and impact of trust multiplies quickly. The employee trusts the CEO. The CEO trusts the employee. The company gets bigger and better things accomplished. Everything happens with greater efficiency. According to the SAM *Advanced Management Journal*, "When managers give group members autonomy, they are sharing control, and this demonstrates a high level of trust in employees. Trust is seen as a reciprocal process, whereby trusting a group and sharing control over group activities inspires trust in return."[4]

## High Trust University

When Nido Qubein took over as president of High Point University, he decided to change the way most colleges view students. He had the inexpensive sturdy wooden couches most colleges use in resident halls and lounges replaced with high-grade leather ones. Older televisions were replaced by the newest flat-screens. The list of upgrades goes on and on, and High Point University is a gorgeous facility today. Many universities might worry that the students would abuse the nicer amenities. Qubein told me, "We have seen the opposite. If you respect people, they will step up. We made this campus absolutely beautiful and the students respect it, tell others about it, and do better academically as a result." He added that, "Trust is fundamental to all we do." The payoff: more students, greater visibility, a better work environment, higher retention and productivity, and a place where pride abounds among students, faculty, and staff.[5]

## Accept the Magnitude of your Risk

The potential benefits of extending trust to others are great, but be prepared to accept the unpredictable results. When our oldest daughter was only two-and-a-half years old, we trusted her to set the dining room table with our good dishes. My wife, Lisa, showed her how to hold the plates with both hands, but more importantly, Lisa showed a willingness to trust and gave an extra big dose of encouragement. Our daughter understood that we entrusted her with something very special, and she proved worthy of that trust. Though our daughter seemed young for the task, we examined the risk and felt the value of instilling confidence in our daughter outweighed the possibility of a broken dish. Although we were prepared for it, she never dropped one.

---

Trust is always a risk.

---

## Trust on the Farm

My dad is masterful at extending trust to others. On the farm we learned to drive the tractors and take care of huge pieces of equipment at a very young age. He often said, "Give your kids as much responsibility as they can handle." The only problem with that notion is that you often don't know how much they can handle until you give them too much. But even that can be a positive learning experience if handled well.

In my early teens, I was trusted to drive a dump truck, fuel up big tractors, and hold the brake down while my dad worked under equipment, where he took the risk of getting run over if I let off the brake pedal. When extended trust, most often I stepped up. But there are always risks when trusting people. One time I ran into our car with the tractor. Another time I pulled up too close to the fuel barrels with the digger, caught the hose, and we lost about four hundred gallons of fuel. In the midst of these major errors, one might think it's not worth it to trust. The most amazing thing is that I remember my dad staying calm in all of these situations. He knew I felt terrible. He moved quickly to a solution and then soon trusted me again. This was powerful.

It's almost like getting back on a horse that has bucked you off. If you don't get back on, the horse might think she can get away with that kind of behavior. How you react hugely impacts their future expectations of themselves.

Dad taught all of his six kids in the same manner. He trusted us, and in turn, we wanted to please him. Dad always said that it was better to trust those who are not worthy of it than to not trust someone who is. By trusting people my dad accomplished much and gained many friends. Even more importantly, that extension of trust became a turning point opportunity for many of those he trusted.

## Trust in Pieces

Although you want to extend trust to people, how much you give should be dependent on how much you think they can handle. In other words, you want to start out with a little, and let things grow from there. When they let you down, find out what went wrong, and repeat the process, just as Dad did on the farm. Extending trust must be coupled with preparation. Let trust be nurtured so that it can grow to maturity. To those who show themselves trustworthy with a little, more responsibility and trust will be extended.

> **Resources for evaluating the trustworthiness of a business:**
>
> 1. *Advice of a few wise friends,* mentors, or business leaders whom you trust.
>
> 2. *The Attorney General's office,* to see if there have been any complaints.
>
> 3. Businesses accredited by the *Better Business Bureau* (www.bbb.org), which generally have commitments to customer service, quality, and high ethical standards.
>
> 4. *Dun and Bradstreet* (www.dnb.com), whose global commercial database contains more than 140 million business records. Their valuable unbiased information helps you make intelligent commercial decisions.
>
> 5. *Angieslist.com,* an online provider of unbiased ratings and feedback.
>
> 6. *Consumer Reports.*

## Beware

Most people can easily think of a time they have been cheated, lied to, or otherwise deceived. Internet and "get-rich-quick" scams are prolific. Humans have a tendency to find ways to take advantage of each other for their own benefit. The examples are found throughout history from the Trojan Horse to the 2 million dollars waiting for you in a faraway bank if you will just pay the interest online.

I'm reminded of the snake, Kaa, in Disney's *The Jungle Book* movie, who slithers up to Mowgli with his hypnotic stare saying, "Trusssst meee," while he slowly winds himself around the boy. Many people and organizations are not worthy of trust, and depending on your experiences, you might find trust difficult. Sometimes we will have to pick up the pieces and move to a solution. But most of the time the increase in productivity, creativity, and responsibility will be worth it in the richness of the relationship as well as in the bottom line.

---

Trust enables risk. Risk sparks innovation. Innovation ups output!

---

## Delegate

Few things make a person feel more valued than asking them to do something important. Can you delegate more significant projects to others? I am not talking about monotonous tasks, nor am I saying you should send them out on the plank without resources and coaching. But consider letting go, and inviting others to take a larger responsibility of the whole process. Let them step up and take more public roles. You will be trusted for it. More trust in them will mean less pressure on you and as a result, a more engaged team.

---

**Apply It!**
What is something significant that you could delegate?

_____

_____

_____

---

## Give Adequate Support and Training

Extending trust gives self-esteem an opportunity to blossom. The best way to bring it to fruition is to give someone a difficult task that they have never done on their own. Make sure they have the resources to accomplish it. Trust them to get it done but don't leave them high and dry if they have a question. Then watch them figure out a way to get it done. They will light up.

## Offer Opportunities for Accountability

Whether it's a direct connection to you or someone else who can be a guide, make sure there are planned progress checks or other avenues for accountability.

## Consider What You're Risking

Money is money, people are people. When it comes to deciding whether to take a risk or not, consider the value of what is being put at risk. For instance, suppose you wanted to sell me an investment property. I would ask some basic questions, and look into background information on the transaction. But even with the best research, I know that land and houses carry risks. No matter how much homework I do, there is always the chance I could lose money. On the other hand, however, imagine you were running a camp or program for my child. Now I would want more than supporting documents and legal guarantees. I might want to find out more about you as a person, or speak to other parents and their children about you and your camp. Losing money may be painful, but my child's safety and well-being are far more important. Evaluate your decision to trust or not to trust according to your priorities.

## Trust Yourself First

In order to extend trust to others you must first be able to trust yourself. It's true. Find someone who does not respect and trust himself, and he will have a hard time extending respect and trust to someone else.

## Keep Promises?

Make and keep personal promises, even if they are small at first. Every commitment a person breaks with herself sucks out a portion of personal trust. Every New Year's Day, millions of Americans do something that harms their own self-esteem and credibility: they make resolutions they don't seriously intend to keep. At first glance, this might seem a little harsh. After all, what's the matter with the traditional New Year's Resolution? It's often insincere. That's the matter. If the January resolutions were sincere, and we gave more than two seconds to plan how we might achieve our resolutions, then the custom would have merit. The damage isn't in the thought; it's in the lack of follow-through. Do you have the same resolution year after year based around these general ideas: spend more time with friends and family, exercise, get out of debt, get organized, and learn something new?

Many Americans, despite their best intentions, abandon their resolutions within weeks. In other words, they've set a goal and did not try very hard to achieve it. Add this to the litany of small promises people routinely make and break, to themselves, and you can easily see why many of us lack self-confidence and determination.

To reverse the trend, make small promises to yourself and keep them. Instead of saying you'll lose 15 pounds by beach season, decide to exercise twice this week. You'll have an easier time following through, and if you keep with it, you'll discover how much easier it is to stay on that kind of path. Remember, it's not the big goals that make the big difference. Rather, it's all the little actions and decisions that will make you the person you'll become. Get into the habit of being truthful with yourself, and you'll find that others will trust you more easily as well.

---

**Your ability to trust yourself
directly impacts your ability to trust others.**

---

Start extending trust wisely today:

- Consider the real impact. Is it just money—or is it lives? The amount of diligence and trust given should be in proportion to the magnitude of the real risk involved.

- Consider the seriousness and frequency of any previous violations. If it was *competence trust*, has that person been trained? If it was *character trust*, has that person expressed a desire to act with integrity?

- Give adequate support and training.

- Offer opportunities for accountability.

- Start by taking small risks. Do it in increments. It is fun, courageous, and most often worth it!

- In order to trust others, you must be able to trust yourself.

# Extending Trust

¶¶¶ Believing in people and trusting them usually brings out their best.

¶¶¶ Trust is a great motivator.

¶¶¶ A culture of trust will improve efficiency and effectiveness.

¶¶¶ Trust inspires more trust.

¶¶¶ Consider the real risk of trusting others. The possible good often outweighs the possible harm in business.

¶¶¶ Be prepared to accept the magnitude of the risk.

¶¶¶ Don't let fear rule your life.

## Ask Yourself ...

1.  If you have been the victim of a scam or a dishonest person, how did you learn to trust others again?

    _____

    _____

    _____

2.  Think of a time when you have been motivated because someone extended trust to you?

    _____

    _____

    _____

    _____

3.  Have you inspired others by extending trust to them?

    _____

    _____

4.  How can you avoid trusting those not worthy of it?

    _____

    _____

    _____

What is expected
of a person will likely be
what they aspire to.

Only when **promises** are kept
can **trust** be rebuilt.

*Chapter Thirteen*

# Rebuilding Trust

## 1111

---

"A single lie destroys a whole reputation of integrity."—Baltasar
Gracián y Morales (1601-1658), Jesuit scholar and philosopher

---

What happens when you need to rebuild trust? What if your
brand—or worse yet, your name—no longer carries any
weight? You have to get it back. To enjoy long-term success, you
must be trusted.

## Plant New Seeds

Remember our trust forest? What do you do if it's been burned down?
You salvage what's left and plant another one. After that, you keep
doing everything you can to let the trees grow while you wait. Any
attempt to build trust too quickly is likely to make things worse.

So what are the seeds of trust? They're small promises—small promises that are kept. That's not just good advice; it is a sound business

strategy. Whether the break of trust was your fault or not, move forward with consistency and integrity. By deciding to act in an honest way, you build esteem and confidence in your family, your organization, your colleagues, and your customers. You also regain self-esteem.

---

To trust yourself and build or rebuild trust with others,
you must make and keep promises.

---

Be cautious with whatever weakness cost you trust in the first place. If you have a habit of missing deadlines, then focus on meeting your deadlines. If you've lost trust because you've done poor-quality work, then look at how to gain the knowledge you need through more education or mentorship. If your integrity or the integrity of your group is under scrutiny, remove secrecy, invite accountability, and adapt a zero-tolerance policy for future indiscretions.

---

"Whoever is careless with the small matters cannot be trusted
with important matters."—Albert Einstein (1879–1955)
Nobel Prize-winning physicist and scientific genius

---

## Brand Trust is Weak

It's difficult to build a trusted brand, because brand trust is generally weak. Why? As Roger Clark, author of *Trust in the Context of e-Business*, says, "Branding focuses very heavily on image—manufacture, manipulation, maintenance. If no relationship is developed and slippage occurs in quality, relevance, or consistency, trust based on branding alone is accordingly brittle." Relationship trust is strong. Brand trust is weak. The more connected the brand is to strong credible relationships or a long consistent history, the stronger the brand will become.[1]

## React-ipedia

When trust is lost, there is little time to lose. Discern the situation, but then quickly make a plan to rebuild it. Wikipedia thrives today because the company made haste to rebuild lost trust after the John Seigenthaler incident.

In November 2005, it came out that an untrue and potentially libelous statement in the biography of John Seigenthaler, a famous journalist, had gone unnoticed for months on Wikipedia. Seigenthaler wrote a fairly scathing editorial in the *New York Times* criticizing Wikipedia as a "flawed and irresponsible research tool."[2]

Since Wikipedia is open-source, meaning it derives its value from the trust people have in it, as the public at large can edit it, this loss of trust was potentially devastating. The Wikipedia Foundation knew that they would need to do more than release an apology to John Seigenthaler. Their actions were as follows:

1.  They made a special section called "biography of living persons," which would be more difficult to edit and would be monitored more frequently.

2.  They stopped allowing anonymous users to create articles.[3]

3.  They spent time showing the relative validity of data in Wikipedia, especially as compared to well-respected encyclopedias.

The preventative and reactive measures taken by Wikipedia in this situation regained their public trust. Further boosting their reputation, *Nature* magazine compared the accuracy of Wikipedia to *Encyclopedia Britannica*, and found them to have roughly an equal number of flaws![4]

## Apologize Thoroughly

When we've wronged someone or broken his or her trust, it's up to us to make it right. This is a big part of rebuilding trust. Part of that is apologizing in a way that satisfies the other person. Sometimes we might say we're sorry and then not get the results we were hoping for. If you aren't sure what will make things right, then ask. Often, the party who has been wronged can tell us what they want. And even if they can't, the act of being heard will often help to diffuse their anger and frustration. Make sure your apology is understood to be sincere and clear. A sincere apology process usually includes the following:

1. I am sorry.

2. That was my fault.

3. What can I do to make it right or solve the problem?

## Forgive and Be Forgiven

One of the easiest ways to be forgiven by people is to let go of your own grudges. If the people around you know you have been willing to bury quarrels in the past, they'll be much more likely to feel the same way towards you. I do not pretend to be a psychologist. And I certainly know forgiveness is not always easy. However, the best marriage advice I ever received was, "Learn to forgive truly and quickly because you are both imperfect." The following tips on forgiveness will go a long way towards rebuilding trust:

- Acknowledge what really happened.
- Acknowledge feelings are truly hurt.
- Be willing to apologize for your role in the matter first.
- Be patient.
- Recognize how much you have been forgiven by others and by God.
- Forgive yourself. Understand that you are not perfect.
- Talk to an uninvolved friend or professional. Do not gossip or speak to someone on the sidelines.
- Give up the need to be right.
- Seek help and accountability to change bad habits.
- Set appropriate boundaries.

## Let It Go

Some mistakes are so big, and some people get so hurt or skeptical, that reconciliation will never be realistic. In those circumstances, do everything you can to apologize for the act that caused their mistrust. But after that, let it go and move on.

## Sharper Image: Money for Nothing

Sometimes a company can go so far in damaging its own trustworthiness, that it's difficult to see any way back. Take the Sharper Image stores for instance. After entering into bankruptcy protection, the gadget and gizmo seller stung customers shortly after a holiday shopping season by announcing that gift cards would no longer be redeemable. The company was treating the plastic as a short-term debt, which would be postponed under their creditor protection plan.

While such a move might be feasible under the law and beneficial to the short-term bottom line, it has undoubtedly left a bad taste in consumers' mouths. After all, gift-givers paid full value for them, only to be told that they were now worthless. The firm announced shortly after that they would begin redeeming cards again, but only if customers spent more than twice the value of the cards on one purchase. Never known for its modest pricing, the company had found another way to save their bottom line. Loyal customers are disappearing, and it is doubtful that Sharper Image will regain the public's trust.[5]

## Go Outside

To rebuild trust, consider going outside your organization. Find someone who can study your situation without bias. It is always a privilege for me to be able to help organizations take steps toward rebuilding trust. By hiring outside counsel, accountants, consultants, or auditors who have no possible conflict of interest, you show a willingness to find and reveal the untainted truth. Any possibility of a vested interest can destroy a growth plan.

## Everyone has a Story

Through an interesting set of circumstances I have become the friend and virtually the guardian of a woman in her late 60s. "Emma" was likely abused as a child, has paranoid schizophrenia, and has seldom trusted anyone. She has very little contact with any family or friends and has lived alone for most of her life. Because she refused medical treatment for a needed procedure, the court ordered that she be put in a psychiatric health center. She resides there with limited free-doms. She is hurt, vulnerable, and extremely suspicious. In the early

PART I

CLARITY

COMPASSION

CHARACTER

COMPETENCY

COMMITMENT

CONNECTION

CONTRIBUTION

CONSISTENCY

PART III

PART IV

PART V

stages of our friendship, she did not trust me, though I was acting out of a desire to help someone in need. She often expressed her fears and obsessions about threats such as Nazis around every corner and various government conspiracy theories.

Three lessons have come out of my 10 years of taking Emma shopping and out for lunch or coffee:

1. Everyone has a story.

2. Over time, trust can be restored and lives enriched.

3. Patience and consistency are essential.

Though it has been a long process, Emma is now showing a small capacity to trust. If I make a commitment to her, I must keep it, even if it's as simple as showing up on time. I have to be understanding and patient. I feel so blessed that she allows me to continue in relationship with her and extends even a little bit of trust now and then. Without trust, there is no basis for a relationship. That is precisely why Emma was so alone in this world. Anyone can learn to trust a little at a time.

## Re-branding After a Disaster

When ValuJet Flight 592 crashed into the Everglades in Florida, so did its company's image and reputation. Up to that point, they had been considered a success story, growing from their 1992 beginnings into a regional powerhouse only three years later, posting a $67 million net profit and being named the top company in Georgia.[6]

But in the aftermath of the tragedy, it was discovered that the airline had practiced poor safety and maintenance techniques, leading to a backlash against its brand, not to mention other discount carriers.

With the public's trust obliterated, the carrier had no option but to fold and merge with Air Tran, another regional airline.

The merger, however, has been successful. As one of the few airlines to make money following the 9/11 downturn, Air Tran has held off larger competitors by following a lean fiscal strategy and sticking to its core business.

In short, the airline has made it, but only after a complete facelift, which in this case included merging with another firm that had a stronger image. Sometimes public trust has been damaged too deeply, and there's simply no way to get it back under the current structure.

---

### 15 Tips To Rebuilding an Organization's Trust

1. Acknowledge the need to address issues.
2. Move quickly to take personal responsibility for your role.
3. Empathetically listen to all involved.
4. Apologize sincerely.
5. Act on a solution or restitution.
6. The more trust has been broken, the larger the re-branding effort.
7. Consider changing the company name—only if you have made real organizational change.
8. If ethical or judgment trust was broken, change leadership.
9. Clarify and share a new trusted vision.
10. Emphasize your commitment to the relationship over the issue.

---

11. Make and keep promises to customers, stakeholders, and the public.

12. Set up accountability to assure promises and rebuilding efforts are completed.

13. Deliver extraordinary and consistent customer service.

14. Make sure systems support rebuilding efforts.

15. Move on.

## Never Burn the Bridge

During my time at K-Life Inc., I had a major difference of opinion with one of my board members. Both of us felt strongly about our positions, and neither one of us was able to change the other's mind. Because of the deadlock, our relationship lost some trust. We just didn't see eye to eye, and it looked like it might affect our relationship for the long term. Given our positions on the board, this disagreement threatened to taint the effectiveness of the board and of the organization.

It would have been easy for either of us to say or do something inappropriate. We both had strong opinions after all. By avoiding gossip and maintaining a healthy respect for each other, our relationship was restored. We both decided not to burn the bridge, and in the end, a restored friendship was the prize.

## Under New Management

We've all driven by a restaurant or other business with a sign that says UNDER NEW MANAGEMENT. Essentially, whoever is running the place is saying, "We know the guy who used to run this business lost your trust, but we'd like the chance to earn it back!" They are trying to distance themselves as far from the previous management as possible.

That's not a bad strategy, if you understand that simply changing the "face" of the company will not be enough without changing the "guts" of it as well. If you change the outside (name or logo) *after* building a trusted inside (quality products or great service), this may be a valid option. When people stop trusting a company, they project that mistrust onto everything associated with it: the products, the people, the services, and so on. One of the best first steps a new manager or owner can take is to show people how much things have changed. In some cases, a new sign or banner out front might do the trick. Other times, the manager might have to dig deeper, like change the company name, logo, and even key personnel.

In politics, challengers to incumbents tout "Change" as their campaign theme because people always seem to want change from the bad things of the previous government. And since the newcomer does not already have a negative track record, spreading the "Change" theme becomes a winning strategy.

If the brand isn't trusted anymore, this is serious trouble. Restorative action must be taken immediately. Make real change. Let the word out that things are different. Deliver and serve the client consistently in the new way and word will get around.

## Rebranding—Right on Target

Target has come a long way since the early 1990s, when it was seen merely as a competitor of Walmart and Kmart. In 2010 *Fortune* magazine ranked Target as 22nd on their list of the world's "Most Admired Companies." Interbrand Design Forum ranked Target as having the second most valuable global brand. *Fast Company* magazine named Target to their list of "Innovation All Stars." And Ethisphere ranked Target among the most ethical companies.[7]

How did Target rebrand themselves? By crafting a branding strategy to become "the hip retailer"—more upscale merchandise, but still at a bargain, to attract younger, more affluent, and educated customers. Now more than 97 percent of Americans recognize their logo—the Target bull's-eye.[8]

Target redesigned their stores to be more attractive to their focused audience—with wider aisles, cleaner fixtures, related departments placed conveniently next to each other, and paintings of categories on easy-to-view signs from the front of the store. Unlike their previous competitors, they don't promote items or services through a public address system, but employees receive incentives for making a product display look great. As a result, Target earned a perfect score of 100 percent on the "Corporate Quality Index and Best Places to Work" survey.[9]

The rebranded Target is hip, fun, colorful, and attracts an eager clientele.

## Rebuilding Trust While Rebuilding a Bridge

In August 2007, a major bridge that crossed the "Mighty Mississippi" collapsed in downtown Minneapolis. Everyone was shocked that such a thing could happen. Thirteen people died in the collapse, many more had major injuries, and an entire state wanted answers.

What about all the other bridges? Why didn't someone know this could happen? What kind of bridge inspections are done by the Minnesota Department of Transportation? A sense of security was lost. Commuters faced detours and delays. Businesses in that area faced economic loss because of poor accessibility.

Mike Zipko, a public relations expert who has dealt with crisis situations, was quoted in a St. Paul *Pioneer Press* article saying, "It takes seconds for a reputation to be impacted in a negative way. It takes a long time, with a lot of little steps along the way, to get it back."

As we look at this rebuilding endeavor, a remarkable effort was made to get the new bridge constructed. Extra energy was put into the timeline, with round-the-clock construction. The contractor used every resource to speed up the process. As a result, the bridge was finished more quickly than promised, and the builders received a bonus of $20 million for getting it done ahead of time. The results went a long way in restoring broken trust.[10]

If you don't enjoy the luxury of being trusted, try going the extra mile. Try over-delivering by doing either more than you promised or by doing it faster than you promised. It will make an unbelievable impression and will give you the number one type of advertising—word of mouth. If you have a proposal that's due in the afternoon, turn it in a couple hours early. Yes, I know if it was that simple, you'd be ahead of schedule every time. The point is this. Do what you have to do in order to overcome mistrust. It might not be easy, but find a way to beat that deadline. Delivering more than expected is a guaranteed way to increase trust.

Little by little, the Minnesota Department of Transportation has regained our trust because of efficiency, speed, and extensive and consistent communication with the public, and outreach to the families and communities. This is a bridge that I take frequently, and I am thankful to be driving that route again. Though I remember the tragedy, my trust is restored.

## A Major Change

When you need to create a major organizational change, you may want to consider the following steps to institute lasting change. The order is important. Do #1 before #2 and so on for lasting change to take hold in your organization.

### 10 Step Process for Instituting Lasting Change

1. Build trust.
2. Create a unified spearhead team.
3. Establish a pressing need for the change to be implemented.
4. Formulate a clear unifying vision.
5. Build and implement a specific strategy.
6. Share the vision often.
7. Enable and equip all shareholders to implement change effort as top priority.
8. Create and recognize improvement, big and small.
9. Deepen change, making sure all systems, policies, and training promote the change.
10. Keep and create systems that foster open communication, listening, reviewing, and adjusting.

# Rebuilding Trust

¶ When we have wronged someone or broken his or her trust, it is our responsibility to make it right.

¶ Trying to rebuild trust too quickly is likely to make things worse, rather than better.

¶ The seeds of trust are the small promises you make and keep.

¶ Stay away from whatever caused you to lose trust initially.

¶ A step toward forgiveness is learning to let go of your own grudges.

¶ At some point after an unaccepted apology, you just have to move on.

¶ When people stop trusting a company, they project that mistrust on everything associated with it: the product, the people, the services, and more.

❦ Sometimes mistrust can only be handled by deep change such as changing the name, logo, or leadership.

❦ Relationship trust is the strongest kind of trust. Brand trust is brittle.

## Ask Yourself ....

1. Can you try to rebuild trust by making small promises—and keeping them?

   _____

2. Do you agree that relationship trust is the strongest form of trust?

   _____

   _____

3. Have you ever made an apology that was not accepted? Was your apology sincere?

   _____

   _____

4. Do you find it difficult to forgive people and move on?

   _____

   _____

5. Does your company need to do some big things to restore trust? If so, what?

   _____

_____

_____

_____

6. Why do some companies bounce back
   quickly when negative publicity strikes and
   others don't?

   _____

   _____

7. What steps would you take to institute lasting
   positive change?

   _____

   _____

   _____

   _____

   _____

   _____

PART I
CLARITY
COMPASSION
CHARACTER
COMPETENCY
COMMITMENT
CONNECTION
CONTRIBUTION
CONSISTENCY
PART III
PART IV
PART V

# PART IV

## DEEP TRUST
## IN A
## FLAT WORLD

Due to the ease of global travel communication, and technology, as well as access to economies and labor forces around the world, we can instantly connect with Thomas Freidman's idea, "The World is Flat." However, "flat" also connotes "shallow" to a large degree. Because we can connect with so many, we have a hard time cultivating depth. Trust at its best is deep. So how do we gain *The Trust Edge* in this flat world?

"Only trust can prevent the geographical and organizational distances of global team members from becoming psychological distances: trust allows people to take part in risky activities that they cannot control or monitor and yet where they may be disappointed by the actions of others."[1]

—Sirkka L. Jarvenpaa and Dorothy E. Leidner, authors and communication experts

*Chapter Fourteen*

# Globalization and Trust

## 1111

"In the broader battle for hearts and minds abroad, we have to be
as good at listening to others as we are at telling them our story.[2]
—Robert Gates, U.S. Defense Secretary

Globalization, the shrinking of borders and broadening of our business horizons, is an enormous component of business today. And consequently, the past couple of decades have seen an explosion in interest of getting business overseas. But for all of the wonderful benefits worldwide commerce brings, it presents an enormous trust challenge. Globalization, outsourcing, changing business models, and the effort to deal across cultures, value systems, and governments, create an ocean of opportunity for suspicion and distrust. Companies looking to expand into new markets would do well to realize that the increased sales, better margins, and dynamic distributions they crave in other countries can only be realized when all parties trust each other. With different languages, cultures, and customs to understand and attend to, that can be a bigger challenge than it seems.

## Guanxi

A good example of how different cultures view business relationships can be seen through Guanxi, the Chinese custom of building relationships. For several centuries, China lacked strong court systems. As a consequence, there was little recourse if someone failed to deliver on their promises or didn't fulfill the terms of their contracts. Businessmen, in turn, took to dealing only with people they knew or those who had strong mutual references. In this way, trust could be established and maintained within commerce. Over time, that tradition has continued. People in many cultures are not used to dealing with strangers, and it can make them uncomfortable. Building trust may start by giving gifts in some cultures, listening in others, and being patient in all.

## International Trust

In Edelman's 2009 global study, the countries that received the highest trust ratings were Brazil, China, The Netherlands, Sweden, India, and Indonesia. Whereas in Australia, Ireland, Italy, France, Germany, and the US, trust in business was the lowest. If trust is low between countrymen, it shouldn't be a surprise that the rest of the world is having trouble trusting the West. Still *The Trust Edge* can be had, and it is well worth the effort.[3]

## IKEA: Trust in Any Language

As was mentioned earlier, IKEA is one of the world's most popular and trusted brands. The Swedish company's success comes from their unique brand of trust. Younger couples, namely, trust the company to deliver high quality, fashionable pieces at affordable prices. As part of their commitment to that demographic, the stores have made it easier for young families to shop. High chairs, strollers, and even supervised playrooms for the kids are all part of the IKEA experience.

Another way that IKEA has secured trust across borders is by keeping control of their consistency. Every product that they sell comes from one of the company stores or through their catalogs. By electing not to use third-party retailers or distributors, IKEA gave up a quick profit in order to keep better tabs on their quality.

The lesson to take from IKEA's success is simple: Being consistent is always in style. And showing your customer you care about their shopping experience will build trust in any language.

"Current polls show that non-governmental organizations (NGOs) are the most trusted and global companies are the least trusted."[4]

## Diversity Boosts Creativity, Undermines Trust

One of the most interesting things I learned in my research on trust is that diversity, one of the biggest buzzwords in modern business and educational institutions, isn't always great for trust. That is, people more easily trust others who are like them, and are more apt to mistrust those who are different. In fact, too much diversity, whether cultural, social, economic, or otherwise, leads to lower levels of trust, which deteriorates productivity and morale. Keep in mind, I do not define "diversity" by color or ethnicity, but rather by ALL of the ways we are each different from one another, such as ways of thinking, backgrounds, political views, and many more.

Be careful. I'm not saying diversity is bad. In fact it is critical to innovation, creativity, and success. The old saying is correct, "If we are both the same, one of us is not needed." So embrace diversity for greater creativity and innovation but consider similarities and opportunities to connect in order to build trust. If ideas, backgrounds, views, and ways of communicating are too diverse, it will affect productivity. It does propose a fine line, but it is evidence worth understanding for effectiveness among work groups and teams.

People are, and always have been, fearful of the unknown. It's the reason we worry most about things we've never seen or done. So when it comes to diversity, a natural reluctance kicks in. When people do not have the same frame of reference, they may not know what to expect from each other. When dealing with someone from a different culture, there is an added layer of mystery about that person or company. Let's find common ground and see how we can develop a trusted atmosphere amidst diversity.

## Trusted Diversity

An obvious microcosm of this idea can be seen in any restaurant serving exotic food to a local population. Most of the American population is comfortable with Chinese takeout or Tex-Mex enchiladas because we are familiar with them, but what about Indonesian or Tanzanian cuisine? Presented with these choices, one may feel trepidation. *Will I like what I order? Is it spicy or mild?* Restaurateurs serving unfamiliar dishes to the larger community know this, and often make a conscious effort to give information about the ingredients and pictures of the dish.

Doing business in new cultures isn't much different. Expect that many aren't going to be familiar with you and might question your values. It would serve you well to be a student of their culture in order to learn their ways of thinking. While I'm not suggesting you attempt to lessen the diversity within your company, it is essential to look at how diversity of any kind can hinder trust.

In building trust globally, we must magnify the Trust Pillars. The global sales person may need to be even more intentional about showing compassion. And he or she must consider questions like, "How do people feel cared for in this culture?" The answer may be much different than our own. For instance, an employee in one culture may feel appreciated with a pay raise, while someone in a different culture may feel much more appreciated with public recognition. The global leader must communicate clearly on the terms of the new culture. Be ready for a paradigm shift. Every culture elevates different values and views of success. Listen. Observe. Learn. In a high-trust climate, differences and diversity are valuable, beautiful, and fruitful.

My brother, Kent, is the President of CSC Arbitrage, a market maker in the commodity industry. His thriving company is made of one person from China, two from India, three from the U.S., and one from Iran. They certainly have a high level of diversity in their company. They are thriving in spite of a poor economy for several reasons. Their environment is built on high expectations, high standards, and high competency. Each is expected to do his or her job well. Second, each person is highly motivated to succeed. New hires are all brought on as paid interns for a specific time. Show you can perform well in the team and earn a job offer. Third, because everyone is so different, they are equals. All (including Americans) are relative minorities, so there is a sense that respect is the only option. Leadership focuses on mission-accomplishing growth activities that emphasize common ground, not differences.

By creating a strong identity that includes shared values and a unifying mission, diverse companies can increase trust, even against the odds. The innovation, respect, and engagement gained leads to trust and a strong bottom line.

As Nick Burns, former U.S. undersecretary of state and professor at Harvard's Kennedy School of Government, points out, "We are in the midst of a major strategic shift in world politics and economics— the rise to power of China, India, Brazil, and others. Business and government leaders in the United States and other Western nations will need to build trusting relationships with their counterparts from these rising countries to achieve effective results."[5]

## Hearst Connects

Cathie Black, President of Hearst Magazines, the world's largest publisher of monthly magazines, continues to garner praise. She has been on *Fortune* magazine's "50 Most Powerful Women in American Business" list each year since it debuted in 1998. Black is responsible for *Good Housekeeping, Popular Mechanics, Cosmopolitan,* and 12 other best-known magazines. Black also heads nearly 200 international editions that reach over 100 countries. How did she accomplish such an aggressive international development strategy? The answer is partnerships. When going international, she attributes success to her team's ability to joint venture. Her strategy is to seek connections with the best native publishing partner she can find. For instance, in breaking into China markets, she partners with IDG and the Chinese Government. According to Black, this ability to compromise, give up some control, and connect has been the secret to Hearst's international success.[6]

## Gestures Matter

While my wife, Lisa, and I were in Japan on business, we had a number of opportunities to observe Asian business practices and note the small differences from our own. Though some differences were slight, if unnoticed or treated with disregard, a foreigner could greatly offend the person with whom they are trying to interact. However, even the slightest effort to adapt to the local Japanese customs was noticed and appreciated.

For example, one afternoon our Japanese hosts offered to act out the common custom of presenting and accepting a business card. In their culture, the card isn't just a piece of paper carrying your contact information; it is a small extension or representation of who you are. In America you'd say thanks and put it in your pocket. In Japan you are expected to read the information carefully before respectfully placing it in your business card case. The giving and receiving of business cards is really a ceremony that ends with bowing until the older person stops bowing.

After taking a few moments to demonstrate the process, our hosts asked another member of our American group to participate in a role-play exercise. She stepped forward into the center of our circle. Our Japanese host produced his card, both gracefully and deliberately. Indifferent to the subtle cultural difference just explained, the American glanced at the card and then shoved it in her purse. The moment was awkward for the rest of us, as we knew she was not showing respect for the Japanese hosts or their culture. The American was showing that it wasn't worth her time and energy to learn about their way of doing things. In spite of this lady's disregard, the Japanese hosts continued to be gracious, but the American lady was not trusted anymore. As the weeks went on, that American was invited to fewer and fewer outings. As a result, she probably didn't have that much fun, and most definitely was not rewarded with the lasting friendships that others of us are enjoying to this day.

> **Tips for global interaction:**
> 1. Be humble.
> 2. Be teachable.
> 3. Be observant.
> 4. Research customs ahead of time. Find out what is expected.
> 5. Listen.
> 6. Be quiet. Most cultures are not as loud as our American culture.
> 7. Be thankful.

You don't have to learn every nuance of a new country you're working in right away, but recognize that the differences are there, and make an effort to learn about them. Show people you care about them, and they'll give you the benefit of the doubt. Ignore their feelings, and you'll never create trust. When my wife and I travel internationally, we try to assume a humble mental posture. The posture, though only in our minds, is that of head bowed, showing humility and a readiness to receive and serve. Getting this image in our heads has served us well in connecting, relating, and building trust globally.

## The American Image

Regardless of how you feel about American foreign policy, it's important to be realistic about other cultures' assessments of us. The fact is that we're very visible. Our movies, our military involvements, and our high-profile news stories have shaped impressions. With that in mind, know that you may have to go the extra mile to win over international associates. It isn't that everyone you meet is going to be anti-American. My experiences have actually been quite the contrary. Most people have welcomed us graciously and are not as skeptical of Americans as some would have you believe. Still, whether good or bad, the United States has a reputation that precedes you. Show people they can trust you, as an American and as an individual, and they most likely will.

## Competence Counts in China

For all the joys of globalization, the same rules of trust still apply. This issue has hit the spotlight over the last couple of years as products from China, which recently eclipsed the U.S. as the world's largest exporter, have proven to be defective, or even deadly.

In fact, Chinese products currently account for roughly 60% of all product recalls within the U.S. today, compared with only 36% in 2000. Some of these mishaps could be attributed to their greater role in manufacturing as well as increased market share. A number of high-profile situations, however, cast light on some of the nation's safety practices.

For instance, in 2008, 300,000 children got sick and eight died from milk that contained melamine. The recall of 60 million cans of pet food arose from reports of organ failure and eventual deaths in cats and dogs. Additionally, 170,000 tubes of toothpaste had to be pulled from shelves when it was determined that they were tainted with a deadly chemical. More than 1.5 million toys were discovered to be unsafe for children because of their lead content and choking risks.

In each case, the companies responsible for the manufacturing and distribution of these products risked hefty lawsuits and suffered an enormous blow to their trustworthiness. In the milk contamination case alone, 11 countries stopped all imports of mainland Chinese dairy products. Increased skepticism, regulation costs, and firings cost countless dollars and *The Trust Edge* for many companies. Making products overseas can be good business, but not if it costs you your reputation at home.[7]

## The Global Economic Crisis

"This is probably the first transformational crisis of our globalized age. Many things will change,"[8] according to Klaus Schwab, founder and Executive Chairman of the World Economic Forum.

We are now in a global economy and the economic crisis of 2008 and 2009 proved it. Across the globe, markets were impacted. As William R. Rhodes, Chief Executive Officer, Citibank NA, said, "What is happening in the markets in the U.S. is affecting the credit markets worldwide."[9]

Trusted leaders must think responsibly about the impact of decisions on the global economy. The failings in the U.S. and Britain are reflected in the new research that puts their banking systems at 40th and 44th place as most trusted in the world. Whose banks are most trusted? Canada is number one, followed by Sweden, Luxembourg, Australia, and Denmark. Who else beats U.S. and U.K. banks? The answer is El Salvador, Peru, Germany, Barbados, Estonia, and Nambia, just to name a few![10]

The U.S. and the U.K. must avoid pride and arrogance. They must consider adopting more transparent accountability if they want to lead the world in economic trust again. George Soros, Chairman, Soros Fund Management LLC remarked, "The present crisis is the end of an era based on the dollar ... and we need a sheriff, we need a new sheriff, not the Washington consensus."[11]

---

"This crisis has proved that the economy is truly global
—and whatever happens in the USA or China
will ultimately affect all global markets."[12]
—H.H. Sheikh Mohammed Bin Rashid Al Maktoum,
Vice-President and Prime Minister of
the United Arab Emirates, Ruler of Dubai

---

## Even in War

There were plenty of lessons learned from the Iraq war. One of them is the philosophy learned in 2007 when a strategic decision changed the focus from fighting the insurgents toward protecting the local population. What happened? The Allied troops built trust with the locals. The locals helped turn the war against the militant groups.

Now in Afghanistan a similar strategy is being used. According to Jim Michaels, the focus will not be on battling insurgents "face-to-face" but rather, "by winning the trust of the local population, one farmer at a time." According to Marine Capt. Mike Hoffman, "The Taliban is not my focus. If I focus on the people, I'll get (rid of) the Taliban or make them irrelevant. I didn't come here to kill bad guys." Their strategy is to help local farmers by putting in wells and giving security. Already, locals have shared where many of the insurgents are located and have showed them where many roadside bombs have been placed. A partnership has begun, and *The Trust Edge* is just beginning to sharpen. Even in a war across cultures, trust is a cornerstone for success.[13]

# Globalization & Trust

¶¶ Get to know people individually rather than stereotyping.

¶¶ When there are cultural differences, be transparent. Let people get to know the real you.

¶¶ People are more likely to trust others who are like them, and less likely to trust those who are different. Do the extra work to increase trust with those who are different than you.

¶¶ As a team leader, find common ground.

¶¶ Ignoring another culture's feelings or customs leads to skepticism, not trust.

¶¶ Show people they can trust you, and most often they will.

¶¶ Making products overseas can be good business, but not if it costs you your reputation at home.

## Ask Yourself...

1.  Are you open to learning the customs of your vendor or customer overseas?

    _____

2.  If you had to travel overseas to a client or vendor, what kinds of things would you do or learn about in preparation for the trip?

    _____

    _____

3.  What does it look like to be humble across cultures?

    _____

    _____

4.  What are the benefits and challenges of globalization?

    _____

    _____

    _____

5.  How can your organization do more to earn trust internationally?

    _____

    _____

In building trust
globally,
we must magnify
the Trust Pillars.

"Broadband access literally transforms the way we live, work, play, and learn by providing unprecedented opportunities for people to communicate and access information, improve education and healthcare, and expand the reach of business."[1]

—John Chambers, chairman and CEO, Cisco USA

*Chapter Fifteen*

# Trust in the Online Age

⌒⎵⎵⎵⌒

---

"82% of consumers cited credibility as their most serious concern
when shopping online."[2] —Council of Better Business Bureaus

---

L ike globalization, the online revolution has brought thousands of
new helps and efficiencies to the way we work. It has drastically
changed the way we do business. But at the same time, e-commerce
has the potential to slow down trust.

That's because the Internet is the ultimate medium in anonymity.
Regardless of what you think, or what others say, you know that
the person or company on the other end of a transaction could be
anyone anywhere. In this environment, distrust is more prevalent.

## The Secret for Amazon and Elance

Amazon.com, the world's largest retailer, understands reputation. In
the process of building an innovative online superstore, they took

a critical step early on that has paid huge dividends: They invite customers to give feedback on their purchases. With every book, CD, and gadget sold, they offer a chance to rate the product and comment on the service they received. Because of this, and because they accept and post the bad with the good, they are able to build trust quickly. Customers trust each other more than they trust marketing propaganda.

---

Over 33% of people that lose trust in a company, openly campaign against that company on the internet.[3]

---

In the online age, reputation moves at the speed of light. Do something wrong, and the public will know about it within minutes. Get it right, and your reputation can skyrocket in a short amount of time. Consider the Amazon.com model of collecting feedback on your own site. It's a risk, but it will show that you are serious about earning the trust of your customers.

Elance, the online freelancing site founded in 2002, believes you must create an environment of rational trust in order to thrive online. They certainly have done just that. Amidst the slew of sites that outsource freelancers from around the world, Elance has become a hit. While it is true that many companies are finding it easier and more cost-effective to outsource work to freelancers, breaking through the suspicion in such an environment has kept most companies in this industry mediocre at best. Companies and freelancers are both wary of trusting in a relationship that begins online. "Will the project get completed?" "Will I get it on time?" "Will I get paid for my work?"

Recognizing that professionals need to have an environment where trust can develop, Elance did four main things to make this happen. First, Elance set a precedent for online escrow accounts held by a third party. This added to the likelihood of getting paid because it can be set up so that part of the escrow is released as each "milestone" in a project is completed, even though the hiring party still gets the final say as to whether the finished project is acceptable. Secondly, they opened communications between hiring party and service provider by offering the ability to message board, chat, and even call a potential provider before hiring them. Third, they made it easy for providers to show previous examples of work. The best indicator of future work is previous work. It makes the hiring company less cautious and more trusting. And finally, like Amazon.com, they set up clear feedback ratings that are dependent on new work for providers. This is not only helpful to the hiring company; it is very motivating to the freelancer.[4]

---

"A brand for a company is like a reputation for a person.
You earn reputation by trying to do hard things well."
—Jeff Bezos, founder and CEO of Amazon.com

---

## TJ Maxx Learns the Hard Way

In 2007, TJ Maxx, a discount retailer with more than 2,500 stores across North America and the United Kingdom, disclosed that it was the victim of the largest hack ever into their corporate computer records. During the cyber-heist, which is still being investigated, it was determined that information from nearly 46 million credit and debit cards was stolen by hackers who accessed the company's internal database. Additionally, nearly half a million records contained even more sensitive information, such as addresses and driver's license numbers.[5]

Because of the technical nature of the theft, and its massive scale, a spokesperson admitted the company "may never be able to know" how much damage has been done. The retailer may have compounded their problems by failing to disclose the breach as quickly as they could have. In fact, a number of lawsuits have been brought by customers who feel the company didn't take adequate measures to protect their data. Some of the consequences follow:

- More than $135 million in charges related to the massive security breach
- Ongoing negative publicity globally
- Share price loss
- A class action lawsuit that could cost tens of millions more.[6]

---

51% of consumers trust Amazon and eBay; 41% trust large retail stores.[7]

---

## Make Guarantees

One of the simplest ways to gain trust online is to make guarantees. Let customers know that you have a return policy if they aren't happy with your products. Put it in writing that you will not share or sell their contact information.

## Use Email Carefully

Email is an indispensable part of business today. But to keep things safe, and your business trusted, adhere to a few guidelines:

- *Be careful in using email to find new business.* Most of the public started realizing how easy it was to fake emails when a few thousand of us started getting urgent requests from the Nigerian minister of finance! Just as bad are the endless spam solicitations that flood our inboxes. All of this has contributed to a hefty amount of skepticism regarding email, so keep that in mind if you use it as a prospecting tool. Don't make outrageous claims, and be sure to post ways for people to easily find out about who you are.

- *Don't send sensitive information.* Email is seldom completely secure, so do not include sensitive information like credit card numbers, account details, and so on.

- *Keep it professional.* Have you ever sent or forwarded an email to the wrong person, and it ended up an embarrassment? Use extreme caution and avoid these situations. If your email communication is always professional, then you'll have nothing to worry about.

- *Understand that it is easier to have miscommunication through email.* So much of communication is in tones and nonverbal cues. Use the phone or meet in person for important or sensitive business. Consider that ALL CAPS could come across like yelling. Finally, don't skip the greeting, "Hello John." We don't start in on our first sentence when someone answers the phone. We say hello and reveal our identity first, then we begin our conversation.

---

62% of online shoppers are concerned about becoming victims of email fraud.[8] —Habeas

---

# Blog Trust?

Blogs are trendy, but not always trusted, as shown below. If you decide a blog is right for you, make it stand out by offering fresh, practical, relevant, and true content.

---

*Fig. 1* **Trusted Information Sources**

How much do you trust the following information sources?

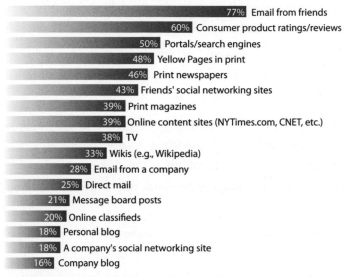

| | |
|---|---|
| 77% | Email from friends |
| 60% | Consumer product ratings/reviews |
| 50% | Portals/search engines |
| 48% | Yellow Pages in print |
| 46% | Print newspapers |
| 43% | Friends' social networking sites |
| 39% | Print magazines |
| 39% | Online content sites (NYTimes.com, CNET, etc.) |
| 38% | TV |
| 33% | Wikis (e.g., Wikipedia) |
| 28% | Email from a company |
| 25% | Direct mail |
| 21% | Message board posts |
| 20% | Online classifieds |
| 18% | Personal blog |
| 18% | A company's social networking site |
| 16% | Company blog |

Source: North American Technographics Media and Marketing Online Survey, 2008[9]

# eBay: Bidding on Trust

eBay is one of the purest icons of trust. The legendary website for home-based buyers and sellers was founded on the very simple idea: people who want to auction their goods could list and sell them to other individuals who want to buy. A trip to any flea market would show that this concept is not revolutionary. But the thing that makes eBay unique and relevant to our discussion is its foundation of trust, even online.

Their business would fall apart without cooperation between buyers and sellers. While a system is in place to deal with cases of fraud, the community is largely self-governing. When bidders win, they send their money and expect sellers to ship their items promptly. And with over 212 million registered users and more than 1.5 billion items sold each year, it seems to be working out well! If the public had not trusted eBay, if fraud were prevalent enough or disagreements frequent enough, buyers would have chosen to look elsewhere for their electronics and household goods. But because of their confidence in each other, as well as eBay's fraud-recovery procedures, the auctions roll on to the tune of $5.97 billion per year.[10]

As the site has grown from a curiosity to an economic giant, fraud has become a bigger issue for eBay. In response, the company has instituted new policies designed to make their operations more buyer-friendly. In return, sellers have threatened to boycott the service. Going forward, it will be interesting to see if eBay can continue to capitalize on consumers' trust while minimizing the effects of dishonesty and suspicion.

Are there similar problems on the horizon for your company? How will you deal with them when they arrive?

---

Online fraud costs $2.6 billion this year.[11]

---

## The Making of a Trusted Online Presence

How might you make your company website more trusted? First "be" trusted by implementing the Eight Pillars in every area of your organization. Then to show that you are trusted, consider the following 15 tips for a trusted site:

1. *Be simple and clear.* Look at Google's site. People use it because it is simple. Cut the distractions. Make sure people clearly understand what you offer.

2. *Be informative.* People want solutions. Give fresh information or concrete ways to solve problems.

3. *Make it easy to connect with you.* Show contact information clearly. Provide a phone number that actually gets answered along with a street address instead of a P.O. Box. It goes a long way to gaining trust with the public when you include multiple ways to genuinely access you.

4. *Show real people.* Pictures that show your people, customers, or offices all help build trust in the anonymous web world. Stories and testimonials can make it even more personal.

5. *Be a member of credible groups and show their logo.* Being a member of the BBB reveals that you have been studied by a trusted, unbiased, outside organization and that you are willing to commit to operating by a code of ethics. Showing that your site is VeriSign protected gives customers buying confidence. Showing the logo of trusted associations or partners gives your site accountability and a foundation for trust.

6. *Show your history.* "Since 1962" shows history and builds credibility.

7. *Use true client testimonials.* The more credible the client, the more trusted the testimonial. Get the permission to use real names and companies. Consider using a few short video testimonials also.

8. *Include a FAQ section.* Anticipate questions that potential customers may have. A Frequently Asked Questions section can engage potential buyers and give them answers that take them to the next level. It will also cut down on the buyer's need to contact you.

9. *Respond quickly.* Expectations are higher for quick responses in the online world. Get back to people quickly on their questions or needs.

10. *Confirm it.* If someone has signed up for a newsletter or bought a product, make sure a confirmation gets sent to them. It will put them at ease to know they just gave their email address to someone who will actually deliver the information promised.

11. *Keep in touch.* After the transaction, let the client know you still care. Capitalize on the recent purchase or inquiry by sending valuable and pertinent information. This also helps them confirm in their mind that they made a good decision in choosing your company. It might bring them back again.

12. *Avoid too much advertising.* Using your site to advertise too much is a turn off. Give real solutions, real value, and real testimonials.

13. *Update often.* People will feel you are active and competent if you are updating your site. An old site dissolves trust.

14. *Have and display a strong privacy policy.* People look for this before they submit their personal information.

15. *Offer a generous return policy.* Where perceived risk is lower, willingness to participate or buy goes up.

# Trust in an Online Age

¶ The public's trust can change quickly.

¶ Customers trust each other more than they trust propaganda.

¶ In an online age reputation moves at the speed of light.

¶ Be smart with your email use.

¶ Create and implement strategies for a trusted online presence.

## Ask Yourself

1. Why does doing business online require more trust?

   _____

   _____

2. What precautions should you take in giving out information?

   _____

   _____

   _____

3. How have eBay, Elance, and Amazon kept such a strong reputation for confidentiality and responsible handling of both customers and providers?

   _____

   _____

   _____

4. What could your organization do to be more trusted online?

   _____

   _____

   _____

# PART V
## COURAGEOUS TRUST

It takes courage to actually build the Pillars and gain *The Trust Edge*. There are challenges to overcome. Discipline and diligence will be necessities. Few teams, families, and companies are willing to do what it takes to enjoy this great advantage. But nothing is more worth it to you or your organization.

Staying sharp
takes a grinder.

*Chapter Sixteen*

# A Sharp and Lasting Edge

## ᛊ 1 1 1 1 ᛢ

---

"He who waits to do a great deal of good at once, will never do anything."—Samuel Johnson (1709-1784)

---

Have you ever tried to use a dull knife? It makes it hard to get the job done, doesn't it? It takes intentionality and time to stop and sharpen the knife. But by doing so, you are prepared for any kitchen task that comes your way. It is the same with your *Trust Edge*. Sharpening it will give you an advantage in your career and life. You'll face less struggle and greater effectiveness. In a recent study, the elderly were asked about their biggest regret in life. What do you think their biggest regret was? For most, it wasn't wishing they had been more successful or even wishing they had spent more time with family. The biggest regret of the elderly was that they did not take enough risks.

Trust is always a risk. Risk can be scary. Risk takes courage. It might seem like a halt in progress to stop and make a genuine connection. It takes discipline to continually build competency. You might get hurt when you give compassion to an unresponsive coworker. It takes guts to risk your job or a relationship by standing up for what you think is right. Lay the groundwork of trust and enable yourself to take risks. Not every risk is going to mean a gold rush. But sustain your attention on the Pillars of Trust and put yourself in the market for a positive return on your risk.

## An Environment of Trust

Mergers and acquisitions are part of corporate life. For most of the workforce, the word *acquisition* is not typically associated with positive images or memories. Because many employees or friends have experienced the pains of going through a merger or acquisition, concern and fear rise at the first hint of such news.

A group of employees at Earth Security Electronics (Earth Security) had a very abnormal experience. When the 16-year-old security company was acquired by the 4-year-old competitor, Skyline Network Engineering (Skyline), many of the Earth Security employees expected to walk into a terrible workplace situation or even to lose their jobs. Instead Operations Manager, Zach Wells, and his colleagues found themselves stepping into an established environment of trust. Rather than feeling like the new owner was "out to get them," they found a man who extended trust to competent people and trusted his new team members. Instead of harboring resources or tools to get their jobs done, they found leaders who genuinely asked for and followed up on their feedback.

I recently visited Skyline and Earth Security at their new offices outside Baltimore. What a trust climate! In my short time with them I asked a few questions and made some uncommon observations. While the owner and CEO was on the phone making a proposal, a team of techies barged into his office, bringing the COO, myself, and a bottle of champagne to celebrate a new technology that had just come together. The night before, the team thought there was no way they could deliver. The celebration was greeted with a smile and lots of pats on the back from the CEO. Where do employees have such a connection to the CEO that they can interrupt him in such a way?

In another conversation, I learned that at a day retreat, the leadership genuinely encouraged some workers to take more family time and days off for the sake of life balance and longevity. For others the leadership offered help for personal problems. For one employee I met, excitement exuded from his smile and words when he compared Skyline and Earth Security's work culture with his previous work environment and boss. Another employee said, "Our leadership has high expectations but they really care about the team, give every needed resource to do our jobs, and celebrate our accomplishments." The leadership recognizes they can make a better organization when they help individuals get better.

Skyline has practiced their *Trust Edge* advantage to achieve superior growth and exceptional employee retention. For the founder, Brian Holsonbake, trust is the only logical way to run a company. He simply does not have the time or tolerance for any other approach. Holsonbake says, "If you have to build a bunch of controls to make sure your people are doing their job and to watch over their shoulders, then what is the point? Doesn't that just mean you hired the wrong people? If you can't hire good enough people and trust them to do their job to the best of their abilities, then why bother being in business? It just would not be worth it for me."

Both Skyline and Earth Security take specific actions to communicate the importance and the expectation of a trust-based environment. It is a major part of the hiring process and the performance management process. The two companies understand that trust happens when words and commitments are equal with actions and delivery. For them trust is not a nebulous "feeling." It is quite simply the result of consistent, positive behaviors practiced over time and therefore completely manageable. Trust is the core of their business strategy.

Anthony Diekemper, the COO of SkyLine, was installed as the CEO of Earth Security as part of the acquisition. I asked Diekemper why trust is so important to the leadership team of the two companies. "Trust is what we call 'the sweet grease.' It is our number one priority in all aspects of our business. You think trust does not affect the bottom line? Leaders who think their only job is to make money are just missing the bigger picture. As executives, we have an obligation to manage with fiscal responsibility, but the way you optimize the financial performance of the company is to have highly engaged employees. They work harder, give more of their discretionary energy, and are happier to be in your company. The foundation of engagement is always trust. We have been able to retain 100% of the Earth Security employees since we acquired the company, and on top of that we have had previous employees approach us about returning because of what they have heard from the current employees. That would simply never happen without trust."

To illustrate his point, Diekemper shared some of the company's results with me.

Below is a chart showing Skyline's sales growth from 2004, most of which came during 2008-2009 in the heart of the recession. From 2005 to year-end of 2008, they experienced 1200% growth.

**Annual Sales Growth**

2004 ............$144,000

2005 ............$800,000

2006 ............$1,500,000

2007 ............$4,000,000

2008 ............$12,000,000

2009 ............$18,000,000[1]

2010 ............$24M projected for year-end

Both Skyline and Earth Security are brimming with the Eight Pillars of Trust: *Clarity, Compassion, Character, Competency, Commitment, Connection, Contribution,* and *Consistency.* The same is true for Southwest Airlines, Warren Buffett, Google, World of Travel, Harley-Davidson, Purpose Design, and Opportunity International. It can be true for you too. While each Pillar is important, the combination of all eight is what makes for a trusted leader and organization.

---

Trust flows from individuals, not organizations.

---

Individuals are the conduit for trust. It's not up to your organization or the responsibility of any one else. Your courage to take action and become trustworthy will be the invitation for others to follow. Keep working to build the Pillars of Trust. Start by laying the first brick. Perservere through the barriers. Be a clear, compassionate, high-character, competent, committed, connecting, contributing, and consistent leader. When you do, you will enjoy the foundation of all genuine and lasting success, *The Trust Edge*.

‖‖

# Five Ways to Sharpen Your *Trust Edge*

 **Book Dave** to energize and inspire your group. See him speak live at www.DaveHorsager.com or www. TheTrustEdge.com.

**2** **Get a baseline on your trust** with our *Trust Temp 360° Assessment*, as well as a practical process to increase it.

**3** **Utilize our *Trust Edge Coaching* program** to help your leaders build the 8 Pillars of Trust and increase morale, retention, innovation, and results.

**4** **Build a culture of trust** through *The Trust Edge Training* and our *Trusted Action Wheel* process that will help you find and solve the REAL problems affecting your organization.

**5** **Read this book in a management group** or book club using the chapter questions and highlights to apply *The Trust Edge* principles.

For questions about any of these strategies or investments:

# 1-800-608-8969
# www.TheTrustEdge.com
# info@TheTrustEdge.com

# References

*Introduction*

1. Doug Miller, President of GlobeScan. Quoted in Press Release 219, World Economic Forum. Retrieved on 22 July 2009 from http://www2.weforum. org/en/media/ Latest%20Press%20Releases/ PRESSRELEASES219.html.

2. Robert F. Hurley, Fordham University. "The Decision to Trust," *The Harvard Business Review*, September 2006. Retrieved on 22 July 2009 from http://harvard-business.org/ product/decision-to-trust/an/R0609B-PDF-ENG (subscription required).

3. Vanessa Hall, Australian management expert and author. *The Truth about Trust—in Business*. Austin, TX: Emerald Book Company, 2004.

*Chapter 1:* **The Trust Edge**

1. John Whitney, Director of the Deming Center for Quality Management at the Columbia Business School. *The Trust Factor: Liberating Profits and Restoring Corporate Vitality.* New York: McGraw-Hill, 1994, front flap.

2. Companies with high trust levels generated total returns to shareholders at almost three times that of companies with low levels of trust, according to WorkUSA: Weathering the Storm: A study of employee attitudes and opinions. Retrieved on 22 July 2009 from http://www.watsonwyatt.com/research/resrendci. asp?id=W-557&page=1.

3. Harvey Mackay, CEO Mackay Envelope Company. "In business, trust is the key," Opinion, *Star Tribune*. Retrieved on 22 July 2009 from http://www.startribune. com/ business/40562577.html.

4. Robert F. Hurley, Fordham University. "The Decision to Trust," *The Harvard Business Review*, September 2006. Retrieved on 22 July 2009 from http://harvard-business.org/product/decision-to-trust/an/R0609B-PDF-ENG, (subscription required).

5. "Redwood Trees—Sequoia Sempervirens." Big Sur Chamber of Commerce. Retrieved on 22 July 2009 from http://www.bigsurcalifornia.org/redwoods.html.

6. From a 1997 survey of business executives by consulting firm Manchester. John Sullivan. "Gain trust by being consistent," *Tech Republic* April 29, 2002. Retrieved on 22 July 2009 from http://articles.techrepublic.com.com/5100-10878_11-1038899.html.

7.  Maureen Minehan. "Restoring Employee—and Investor—Confidence." Strategy@ Work Article, Watson Wyatt Worldwide. Retrieved on 22 July 2009 from http://www.watsonwyatt.com/strategyatwork/article.asp?articleid=10424&date=September%202002.

## Chapter 2: Impact of Trust

1.  Marilyn Carlson Nelson, Chairman and CEO, Carlson Companies. Quoted in front matter of *The Speed of Trust* by Stephen Covey and Rebecca Merrill. New York: Free Press, 2006.

2.  Peter Bregman. "Why Small Companies Will Win in This Economy," *How We Work*. Harvard Business Publishing. Retrieved on 22 July 2009 from http://blogs.harvardbusiness.org/ bregman/2009/03/why-small-companies-will-win-i.html.

3.  Permission granted for publication from Jason Kottke. Retrieved on 22 July 2009 from http://kottke.org/ 03/07/business-lessons-donut-guy.

4.  "Developing Trust in Leaders: an Antecedent of Firm Performance," SAM *Advanced Management Journal*, 2008. Retrieved on 22 July 2009 from http://goliath.ecnext.com/coms2/gi_0199-7741541/Developing-trust-in-leaders-an.html.

5.  Richard Edelman. "Trust Barometer," 2005. Retrieved on 22 July 2009 from http://www.edelmanapac.com/index.jsp?series=3&article=28&pt=1&year=2005. Also see http://www.edelman.com/trust/.

6.  Jeffrey H. Dyer and Wujin Chu. "The Economic Value of Trust in Supplier-Buyer Relationships," *DSpace*, November 3, 1997. Retrieved on 22 July 2009 from http://hdl.handle.net/1721.1/1439.

7.  Charles H. Green, executive educator and co-author. *The Trusted Advisor, Trust in Business: The Core Concepts*. Trusted Advisor Associates. Retrieved on 22 July 2009 from http://trustedadvisor.com/cgreen.articles/38/Trust-in-Business-The-Core-Concepts.

8.  Jill M. D'Aquila. "Tallying the Cost of the Sarbanes-Oxley Act." *The CPA Journal*. Retrieved on 22 July 2009 from http://www.nysscpa.org/cpajournal/2004/1104/perspectives/p6.htm.

9.  Susan M. Heathfield. "How to build a teamwork culture: Do the hard stuff," *About.com*. Retrieved on 22 July 2009 from http://humanresources.about.com/od/involvementteams/a/team_culture.htm.

10. Edelman is the world's largest independent public relations firm employing 3,200 employees in 53 offices globally. The 2009 Barometer is the firm's 10th study of trust. The findings were compiled from 30-minute surveys of 4,475 people in 20 countries on 5 continents. *Edelman's 2009 Trust Barometer*. Edelman's research firm StrategyOne. Retrieved on 23 July 2009 from http://www.edelman.com/trust/2009.

11. Dennis Stauffer. "An Opportunity to Build Trust," The E-zine of Innovative Leadership. Retrieved on 26 March 2009 from http://www.insightfusion.com/z-zine5-6.htm.

12. Author interview with Valerie McKay, Senior Loan officer of Mortgage & Investment Consultants, April 25, 2009. www.valmckay.com.

13. Tom Kirkendall. "That pesky trust-based business model," *Houston's Clear Thinkers*. Retrieved on 22 July 2009 from http://blog.kir.com/archives/2008/03/ that_pesky_ trus.asp.

14. Bill Otis, former Chief of the Appellate Division in the U.S. Attorney's Office. Quoted by John Hindebraker, "A Counterpoint, from Jeremiah." Power Line Weblog, March 12, 2009. Retrieved 22 July 2009 from http://www.powerlineblog. com/archives/2009/03/023044.php.

15. Christine Lagarde, Minister of Economy, Industry, and Employment of France. Quoted in an official summary of *A Roadmap Out of the Economic Crisis*, World Economic Forum. Retrieved 22 July 2009 from http://www. weforum.org/en/ knowledge/KN_SESS_SUMM_27383?url=/en/knowledge/ KN_SESS_SUMM_27383.

16. Richard Edelman, CEO of Edelman, the world's largest public relations firm. Statement on release of Edelman's 2009 Trust Barometer by Edelman's research firm, StrategyOne. Retrieved on 22 July 2009 from http://www.edelman.com/trust/2009.

17. Stefan Molyneux. Author interview on May 5, 2009. Pre-interview podcast from the 2009 New Hampshire Liberty Forum, May 7, 2009. Retrieved on 22 July 2009 from http://cdn4.libsyn.com/ftl/FTL2009-03-06.mp3.

18. Roger Yu. "Airlines score lower than IRS in customer satisfaction," *USA Today*, March 19, 2008. Retrieved on 22 July 2009 from http://www.usatoday.com/travel/ news/2007-05-15-airline-survey-usat_N.htm.

19. *Southwest Airline Fact Sheet*. Southwest Airlines. Retrieved on 22 July 2009 from http://southwest.com/about_swa/ press/factsheet.html.

20. Werner Haas. "How Southwest Airlines Plans for Success," *Associated Content*. Retrieved on 22 July 2009 from http://www.associatedcontent.com/article/ 134537/ how_southwest_airlines_plans_for_success_pg2.html.

21. Christopher Elliott. "Why Cut-rate carriers are No. 1. Travelers consistently favor Jet Blue and Southwest…but why?", MSNBC, March 17, 2008. Retrieved on 22 August 2009 from http://www.msnbc.msn.com/id/23526154/ns/travel-tips/.

## Chapter 3: Barriers to Overcome

1. *Edelman's 2009 Trust Barometer*. Edelman's research firm, StrategyOne. Retrieved on 22 July 2009 from http://www.edelman.com/trust/2009.

2. Watson Wyatt survey of 13,000 people in varied job levels and industries. Shari Cuadron. "Rebuilding Employee Trust," *WorkForce*, October 2002, January 17, 2002.

3. Yankelovich has been a respected research firm since 1958 specializing in global trends and futures. "Industry Statistics," *Bazaarvoice*. Retrieved on 22 July 2009 from http://www.bazaarvoice.com/industryStats.html.

4.  Lisa Bevere. *Nurture.* New York: Faithwords, 2008, p. 220.

5.  Robert F. Hurley, Fordham University. "The Decision to Trust," *The Harvard Business Review,* September 2006. Retrieved on 22 July 2009 from http://harvard-business.org/product/decision-to-trust/an/R0609B-PDF-ENG.

6.  Carl Weiser. "Survey: Young people losing trust in government," *USA Today,* January 1, 2004. Retrieved on 22 July 2009 from http://www.usatoday.com/news/politicselections/nation/2004-01-16-youngvoters-gns_x.htm.

7.  Harvard Political Scientist Robert Putnam's epic study on diversity. Michael Jonas. "The downside of diversity," *The Boston Globe,* August 5, 2007. Retrieved on 22 July 2009 from http://www.boston.com/news/globe/ideas/articles/ 2007/08/05/the_downside_of_diversity/.

8.  Janet Presser. *Humility Breeds Trust.* New York: Executive Excellence Publishing, 2006, p. 8.

## Chapter 4: Pillar One–Clarity

1.  Harvey Mackay, CEO Mackay Envelope Company. "In business, trust is the key," Opinion, *Star Tribune.* Retrieved on 22 July 2009 from http://www.startribune. com/ business/40562577.html.

2.  *Edelman's 2009 Trust Barometer.* Edelman's research firm, StrategyOne. Retrieved on 22 July 2009 from http://www.edelman.com/trust/2009.

3.  Proverbs 29:18, *The Holy Bible,* King James Version. New York: American Bible Society: 1999.

4.  "The Missing Link: Driving business results through pay for performance," *HP Insider Series,* 2007. Retrieved on 22 July 2009 from http://i.i.com/cnwk.1d/ html/itp/successfactors_P4PGuide.pdf.

5.  Joe Murtagh. "Lessons from a Thriving Walmart and failed Kmart," The DreamSpeaker, Business Journal Columns—Marketing. Retrieved on 22 July 2009 from http://www.thedreamspeaker.com/lessons-from-a-thriving-wal-mart-and-failed-kmart/.

6.  Nohria Nitin, William Joyce, and Bruce Robertson. "What Really Works," *Harvard Business Review,* July 2003, pp. 42-53.

7.  Matt Asay. "Google's market share tops 65 percent," *The Open Road, CNet.com.* Retrieved on 22 July 2009 from http://news.cnet. com/8301-13505_3-9838695-16.html.

8.  "Company Overview, Coporate Information," *Google.* Retrieved on 22 July 2009 from http://www.google.com/corporate/.

9.  "IKEA History," *IKEAFans.* Retrieved on 22 July 2009 from http://www.ikeafans. com/ikea/ikea-history/ikea-history.html.

10. Dan Amira, "Who Is the New Most-Trusted Person in America?" Daily Intel, July 20, 2009. Retrieved on 22 July 2009 from http://nymag.com/daily/intel/2009/07/who_is_the_new_most_trusted_pe.html

11. "The C-SPAN Mission." Retrieved on 22 July 2009 from http://www.c-span.org/about/company/index.asp

12. Elizabeth Cosgriff. "An Interview on 'The Paradox of Choice' with Barry Schwartz," *Open Spaces Magazine*. Retrieved 5 August 2010 from http://www.open-spaces.com/article-v8n4-schwartz.php.

13. Sheena S. Iyengar and Mark J. Lepper. "When Choice is Demotivating: Can One Desire Too Much of a Good Thing?" *Journal of Personality and Social Psychology.* Volume 79, Number 6, 995-1006.

14. Lisa Schmeiser. "Costco and the Paradox of Choice," *Seattle Pi Business.* Retrieved on 5 August 2010 from http://www.seattlepi.com/business/417559_costco30.html.

15. Doug Schoen. *Edelman's 2009 Trust Barometer.* Edelman's research firm, StrategyOne. Retrieved on 22 July 2009 from http://www.edelman.com/trust/2009.

16. Antonio Martins de la Cruz. *Edelman's 2009 Trust Barometer.* Edelman's research firm, StrategyOne. Retrieved on 22 July 2009 from http://www.edelman.com/trust/2009.

17. "The Communication Process," The *Importance of Effective Communication*, 2008. Retrieved on 22 July 2009 from http://www.scribd.com/doc/3895068/The-Importance-of-Effective-Communication.

18. "The Communication Process," The *Importance of Effective Communication*, 2008. Retrieved on 22 July 2009 from http://www.scribd.com/doc/3895068/The-Importance-of-Effective-Communication.

19. "The Importance of Reading Non-Verbal Cues," The *Importance of Effective Communication*, 2008. Retrieved on 22 July 2009 from http://www.scribd.com/doc/ 3895068/The-Importance-of-Effective-Communication.

20. Michael Stuart Kelly. *Objectivist Living*, November 2007. Retrieved on 22 July 2009 from http://www.objectivistliving.com/forums/index.php?showtopic=4982

## Chapter 5: Pillar Two–Compassion

1. Robert Moment, author and marketing expert. "Cultivating the Trust Factor," *LeaderValues*. Retrieved on 22 July 2009 from http://www.leader-values.com/Content/detail.asp?ContentDetailID=920.

2. Richard Edelman, President and CEO of the world's largest independent PR firm and trust researcher. *Edelman's 2009 Trust Barometer.* Edelman's research firm, StrategyOne. Retrieved on 22 July 2009 from http://www.edelman.com/trust/2009/.

3. Walter Wink. "Globalization and Empire: We Have Met the Evil Empire and It is US," *Political Theology*, (2004) 5:3, p. 298.

4. H.R.H. Crown Prince Haakon of Norway, Annual Meeting of the New Champions, World Economic Forum. Retrieved on 22 July 2009 from http://www.weforum.org/en/events/ArchivedEvents/AnnualMeetingoftheNewChampions2008/index.htm.

5. *Keeping the People Report* (E-Letter), Volume 13, Spring Issues, 2008. Retrieved on 22 July 2009 from http://www.keepingthepeople.com/newsletter/vol-13-spring-2008.html.

6. Retrieved on 22 July 2009 from http://www.fedsmith.com/article/1329/when-bad-supervisors-happen-good-people-price.html.

7. "Health care takes its toll on Starbucks" (Associated Press), MSNBC—Business. Retrieved on 22 July 2009 from http://www.msnbc.msn.com/id/9344634.

8. Nohria Nitin, William Joyce, and Bruce Robertson. *What Really Works: The 4 plus 2 Formula for Sustained Business Success.* New York: HarperCollins, 2003.

9. "America's Best Leaders," *US News and World Report,* December 1-8, 2008, p. 49.

10. Joe Love. "Energize Your Organization with Motivating Rewards," Ezine@rticles. Retrieved on 23 July 2009 from http://ezinearticles. com/?Energize-Your-Organization-With-Motivating-Rewards&id=2024864.

11. Tom Rath and Donald Clifton. *How Full Is Your Bucket? Positive Strategies for Work and Life.* New York: Gallup, 2004, p. 40.

12. Tom Rath and Donald Clifton. *How Full Is Your Bucket? Positive Strategies for Work and Life.* New York: Gallup, 2004, p. 30.

13. *Keeping the People Report* (E-Letter), Volume 13, Spring Issues 2008. Retrieved on 22 July 2009 from http://www.keepingthepeople.com/newsletter/vol-13-spring-2008.html.

14. March Schoofs. "Giving It Away: An American Pharmaceutical Giant Offers to Donate an AIDS Drug to South Africa," *VillageVoice.* Retrieved on 23 July 2009 from http://www.thebody.com/content/art2773.html.

15. "669 Homeowners Sue State Farm for Denying Katrina Claims." (Associated Press), *FOXNews.com,* May 10, 2006. Retrieved on 23 July 2009 from http://www.foxnews.com/story/0,2933,194877,00.html.

16. The Nobel Foundation. *Biography, Mother Teresa, The Nobel Peace Prize 1979.* Retrieved on 23 July 2009 from http://nobelprize.org/nobel_prizes/peace/laureates/1979/teresa-bio.html.

## Chapter 6: Pillar Three–Character

1. Tom Hill, president and chairman of the board at Kimray. *Workforce, Character First!* Retrieved on 23 July 2009 from http://www.characterfirst.com/workplace.

2. Gary Lear. *The Importance of Trust to Organizational Success.* Retrieved on 23 July 2009 from http://www.rds-net.com/Articles/Importance%20of%20Trust.pdf.

3. Socrates, Greek philosopher in Athens (469 BC–399 BC). Retrieved on 23 July 2009 from http://www.quotationspage.com/quote/3584.html.

4. Joel Belz. "Character Counts," *World Magazine.* Retrieved on 23 July 2009 from http://www.worldmag.com/articles/14456.

5. M. E. Greer, President of the American Society of Safety Engineers. "Trust seals leadership," *Professional Safety,* 47(5), 8. Retrieved on 23 July 2009 from http://www.allbusiness.com/11427675-1.html.

6.  *Character, QC Inspection Services.* Retrieved on 23 July 2009 from http://www.qcinspect.com/article/character.htm.

7.  *Character, QC Inspection Services.* Retrieved on 23 July 2009 from http://www.qcinspect.com/article/character.htm.

8.  Elizabeth Dole. "Stepping Stones to Success," *Performance Magazine*, Vol. 13, Issue 4, 2005, p. 34.

9.  Roger M. Boisjoly. "Ethical Decisions-Morton Thiokol and the Challenger Disaster." Online Ethics Center, May 15, 2006. Retrieved on 22 July 2009 from http://www.onlineethics.org/cms/9620.aspx. Also, Engineering Ethics. "The Space Shuttle Challenger Disaster." Department of Philosophy and Department of Mechanical Engineering, Texas A&M University. Retrieved on 22 July 2009 from http://ethics.tamu.edu/ethics/shuttle/shuttle1.htm

10. *Edelman's 2009 Trust Barometer.* Edelman's research firm StrategyOne. Retrieved on 23 July 2009 from http://www.edelman.com/trust/2009.

11. Inspired in part by Dennis Prager's thoughts on Good. See Dennis Prager, *Happiness Is a Serious Problem: A Human Nature Repair Manual.* New York: Reagan Books, 1998.

12. "Honesty: Still the Best Policy. Survey Shows Integrity in Job Candidates More Important Today Than Five Years Ago." October 29, 2002. Retrieved on 22 August 2009 from http://www.roberthalffinance.com/PressRoom?id=277

13. Susanna Hamner and Tom McNichol. "Ripping up the rules of management—Whole Foods CEO John Mackey," *CNN Money.com.* Retrieved on 23 July 2009 from http://money.cnn.com/galleries/2007/biz2/0705/gallery.contrarians.biz2/3.html.

14. Gian Fiero. "The Importance of Standards," *Ezine @rticles.* Retrieved on 23 July 2009 from http://ezinearticles.com/?The-Importance-of-Standards&id=1851824.

15. John Boe. "The Power of Belief and Expectation," *Accomplish Life.* Retrieved on 23 July 2009 from http://www.accomplishlife.com/articles/120/1/The-Power-of-Belief-and-Expectation/Page1.html.

16. Author interview with Joe Kimbell, owner of World or Travel Inc., on March 10, 2009.

17. Meirine Giggins. "Concerning the Market," *Business Report,* February 18, 2007. Retrieved on 23 July 2009 from http://www.busrep.co.za/ index.php?fSectionId=18 69&fArticleId=3685967.

18. Philippa Foster Black, director of the Institute of Business Ethics. Quoted in Robert Moment, *The Seven Principles of Business Integrity,* Scribd. Retrieved on 23 July 2009 from http://www.scribd.com/doc/2526856/The-7-Principles-of-Business-Integrity.

19. "Vision, Mission, and Values," The Better Business Bureau. Retrieved on 23 July 2009 from http://www.bbb.org/us/mission-and-values.

20. Robert F. Hurley, Fordham University. "The Decision to Trust," *The Harvard Business Review,* September 2006. Retrieved on 22 July 2009 from http://harvardbusiness.org/product/decision-to-trust/an/R0609B-PDF-ENG (subscription required).

21. American Management Association, 2002. T. McCollum. "Ethics Escapes Corporate Practice," August 2002. Retrieved on 22 August 2009 from http://findarticles.com/p/articles/mi_m4153/is_4_59/ai_90257853/.

22. Leslie Wilk Braksick. *Unlock Behavior Unleash Profits.* New York: McGraw-Hill, 2007, p. 213.

*Chapter 7:* **Pillar Four–Competency**

1. Miguel Helft. "Google's Market Share Grows and Grows and Grows," *The New York Times,* December. 28, 2007. Retrieved on 23 July 2009 from http://bits.blogs.nytimes.com/2007/12/28/googles-market-share-grows.

2. Tanvir Orakzai. "US Auto Industry Decline Lessons from Ford and GM," *American Chronicle,* July 4, 2007. Retrieved on 23 July 2009 from http://www.american-chronicle.com/articles/view/11242.

3. Joe Murtagh. "Successful Organizations Must Meet the Challenge of Change," County Business Journal Publications (2001): 6.

4. Peter Vaill. *Learning as a Way of Being.* San Francisco: Jossey-Bass, 1996, p. xv, p. 188.

5. Proverbs 13:20, The Holy Bible: New international Version. Kenneth Barker, gen. ed. Grand Rapids: Zondervan, 2002.

6. Zig Ziglar. "Using your time," Entrepreneur Article, *Evan Michael Motivation and Strategies for Entrepreneurs.* Retrieved on 23 July 2009 from http://www.evancarmichael.com/Entrepreneur-Advice/448/Using-Your-Time.html.

7. "Television Statistics," *Television and Health, TV-Free America.* Retrieved on 23 July 2009 from http://www.csun.edu/science/health/docs/tv&health.html#tv_stats.

8. Albert van Zyle. "10 Ways History's Finest Kept Their Focus at Work," *LifeDev.* Retrieved on 23 July 2009 from http://lifedev.net/2008/03/10-ways-historys-finest-kept-focused-at-work.

*Chapter 8:* **Pillar Five–Commitment**

1. Courtney Dench. "Caterpillar to Cut Executive Pay, Sets Hiring Freeze," *Bloomberg.com.* Retrieved on 23 July 2009 from http://www.bloomberg.com/apps/news?pid=20601087&sid=ay_3MtQjV0H0&refer=home.

2. Julie Hirschfeld Davis. "Lehman's Golden Parachutes Were Being Secured While Execs Were Pleading For Federal Rescue," October 6, 2008. Retrieved 22 July 2009 from http://www.huffingtonpost.com/2008/10/06/lehmans-golden-parachutes_n_132258.html.

3. Del Jones and Edward Iwata. "CEO pay takes a hit in bailout plan," *USA Today*. Retrieved on 23 July 2009 from http://www.usatoday.com/money/companies/management/2008-09-28-executive-pay-ceo_N.htm.

4. Luisa Beltran. "WorldCom files largest bankruptcy ever," *CNN Money*, July 22, 2002. Retrieved on 23 July 2009 from http://money.cnn.com/2002/07/19/news/worldcom_bankruptcy/.

5. Susan M. Heathfield. "Trust Rules: The Most Important Secret About Trust," *About.com*. Retrieved on 23 July 2009 from http://humanresources.about.com/od/workrelationships/a/trust_rules_2.htm.

6. Mitchell Brown. "Major Events in the Life of Dr. Martin Luther King, Jr." King Center, Louisiana State University, LSU Libraries, 1994.

7. "From 1903 Until Now." Retrieved on 22 August 2009 from http://www.harley-davidson.com/wcm/Content/Pages/H-D_History/history.jsp?locale=en_US. Also from http://en.wikipedia.org/wiki/Harley-Davidson.

8. Ned Davis Research. "If Only I had Bought…" cover story, *USA TODAY*. April 24, 2007. Also retrieved on 22 August 2009 from http://www.usatoday.com/money/top25-stocks.htm.

9. "US Sub Captain Admits Responsibility," *BBC News*, March 20, 2001. Retrieved on 5 March 2008 from http;//news.bbc.co.uk/2/hi/Americas/1232424.stm.

10. Susan M. Heathfield. "Trust Rules: The Most Important Secret About Trust," *About.com*. Retrieved on 23 July 2009 from http://humanresources.about.com/od/workrelationships/a/trust_rules_2.htm.

11. "Arizona Cardinals, Team QuickBits," *FFMasterMind.com*. Retrieved on 23 July 2009 from http://www.ffmastermind.com/teambits.php?team=ARI.

12. "Ex-NFL star Tillman makes 'ultimate sacrifice.' Safety, who gave up big salary to join Army, killed in Afghanistan," NBC, *msnbc.com and news services*. April 26, 2004. Retrieved on February 20, 2008 from http://www.msnbc.msn.com/id/4815441.

*Chapter 9:* **Pillar Six–Connection**

1. See www.MarketingSherpa.com. July 2007. Retrieved on 22 July 2009 from http://www.bazaarvoice.com/resources/stats.

2. Leslie Wilk Braksick. *Unlock Behavior Unleash Profits*. New York: McGraw-Hill, 2007, p. 214.

3. Richard Branson. "26 Most Fascinating Entrepreneurs," *Inc.com*. Retrieved on 23 July 2009 from http://www.inc.com/magazine/20050401/26-branson.html.

4. Scott Reeves. "Caribou Coffee's Robust IPO" September 23, 2005. Retrieved on 22 July 2009 from http://www.forbes.com/2005/09/23/cariboucoffee-IPO-equities-cx_sr_0923ipooutlook.html.

5. Patricia Fripp, from author interview March 2008 at Presentation Lab for National Speakers Association conference. Also see www.fripp.com.

6. Harish Manwani, president for Asia, Africa, Central and Eastern Europe, Unilever. Annual Meeting of the New Champions, World Economic Forum. Retrieved on 22 July 2009 from http://www.weforum.org/en/events/ArchivedEvents/ AnnualMeetin goftheNewChampions2008/index.htm.

7. Author interview with Kent Horsager, CEO of Compass Strategic Investments, LLC, July 2008.

8. Bruce Francis, vice president of strategy for Salesforce.com. Retrieved from http://news.cnet.com/8301-1023_3-9989019-93.html.

9. Patrick Lencioni, *Overcoming the Five Dysfunctions of a Team: A Field Guide for Leaders, Managers and Facilitators.* San Francisco, CA: Jossey-Bass, 2005.

10. "Building trust in your small business." 2007 Harris Interactive poll Intuit. Retrieved on 23 July 2009 from http://smallbusiness.intuit.com/news/Acquiring-customers/ 18910303/Building-Trust-in-Your-Small-Business.jsp.

11. Peter Bregman. "Why Small Companies Will Win in This Economy," *How We Work, Harvard Business Publishing.* Retrieved on 22 July 2009 from http://blogs. harvardbusiness.org/bregman/2009/03/why-small-companies-will-win-i.html.

12. Michael Ogrizek, Managing Director and Head of Communications at the World Economic Forum. Quoted in Press Release 219, *World Economic Forum.* Retrieved on 22 July 2009 from http://www2.weforum.org/en/media/ Latest%20Press%20Rel eases/PRESSRELEASES219.html.

13. Mark A. Zasadny. Blog/email written 28 August 2008. Used with permission.

## Chapter 10: Pillar Seven–Contribution

1. Mark LeBlanc. "Growing Your Business." Retrieved on 23 July 2009 from http://www.smallbusinesssuccess.com.

2. Background retrieved from http://en.wikipedia.org/wiki/History_of_IBM and from www.ibm.com.

3. Background retrieved from http://www.google.com/search?q=walmart+history&ie =utf-8&oe=utf-8&aq=t&rls=org.mozilla:en-US:official&client=firefox-and www. walmart.com.

4. Brian Tracy. "Eat That Frog," *Scribd.com.* Retrieved on 23 July 2009 from http://www.scribd.com/doc/4004390/Brian-Tracy-Eat-That-Frog.

5. Day-Timer Inc Survey. 2009. Retrieved on 22 July 2009 from http://www.daytimer. com/Time-Management-Resources/Adults-and-their-Time/0/False.

6. Jonathan B. Spira. "The Cost of Not Paying Attention." Basex Research, 2005. Quoted in Time Management Statistics, Key Organization Statistics. Retrieved on 23 July 2009 from http://www.keyorganization.com/time-management-statistics. php.

7.  Institute of Psychiatry study at the University of London. *Yoga Journal*, p. 22, 12/2005. Retrieved on 22 July 2009 from http://www.keyorganization.com/time-management-statistics.php.

8.  Lisa Belkin. "Time Wasted? Perhaps It's Well Spent," *The New York Times*, May 31 2007. Retrieved on 23 July 2009 from http://www.nytimes.com/2007/05/31/fashion/31work.html.

9.  Donald Whetmore. "Time Management Facts and Figures," 2009. Retrieved on 22 July 2009 from http://www.dovico.com/time-management-factsandfigures.html.

10. Del Quentin Wilber. *The Washington Post*, January 28, 2008. Retrieved on 23 July 2009 from http://www.redding.com/news/2008/jan/28/2007-flight-delays-add-over-170-years-lost-time.

11. Hal Bowman. *Computer Waiting Games: Things to Do While Uploading, Downloading, Processing or Crashing—Activities for the Impatient.* Quirk Books, US, Spi edition, spiral-bound, September 12, 2002.

12. Gloria Mark and Victor Gonsalex, researchers. For Basex. University of California, Irvine. Retrieved on 22 July 2009 from http://www.keyorganization.com/time-management-statistics.php.

## Chapter 11: **Pillar Eight–Consistency**

1.  Stephen Covey. *The 8ᵗʰ Habit*. New York: Free Press, 2004.

2.  "The FedEx Story," *About FedEx*, Fed Ex. Retrieved on 23 July 2009 from http://fedex.com/mx_english/about/story.html.

3.  Tom Rath and Barry Conchie. *Strength Based Leadership*. New York: Gallup Press, 2009, p. 87.

4.  Duffy Robbins. *Hot Talks (Youth Specialties)*. New York: Zondervan, 1987.

5.  James L. Garlow. *The 21 Irrefutable Laws of Leadership Tested by Time*. Nashville: Thomas Nelson, 2002, p. 44.

## Chapter 12: **Extending Trust**

1.  Author interview with Opportunity International. Also retrieved on 16 August 2010 from http://www.opportunity.org/.

2.  "Sir Charles Provides Another Great Story," *Catch Central Florida*. Retrieved on 23 July 2009 from http://catchcentralflorida.com/2008/07/25/sir-charles-provides-another-great-story.

3.  R. Cooper and A. Sawaf. *Executive EQ*. London: Orion Books, 1997.

4.  "Developing trust in leaders: An antecedent of firm performance," SAM *Advanced Management Journal*, 2008. Retrieved on 23 July 2009 from http://goliath.ecnext.com/coms2/gi_0199-7741541/Developing-trust-in-leaders-an.html.

5.  Author interview with President Nido Qubein in May 2009.

## Chapter 13: **Rebuilding Trust**

1. Roger Clark. "Trust in the Context of e-Business." Retrieved 20 July 2008 from http://www/ami/edi/ai/people/Roger.Clarke/EC/Trust.html.

2. Katherine Seelye. "Snared in the Web of a Wikipedia Liar," *The New York Times*, December 4, 2005. Retrieved on 23 July 2009 from http://www.nytimes.com/ 2005/12/04/weekinreview/04seelye.html.

3. Burt Helm. "Wikipedia: A Work in Progress," *BusinessWeek*, December 14, 2005. Retrieved on 23 July 2009 from http://www.businessweek.com/technology/ content/dec2005/tc20051214_441708.htm?chan=db.

4. James Giles. "Internet encyclopedias go head to head," Special Report, *Nature*, December 14, 2005. Retrieved on 23 July 2009 from http://www.nature.com/ news/2005/051212/full/438900a.html.

5. "Sharper Imagine Gift Cards in Court" (Bloomberg). *The New York Post*, March 8, 2008. Retrieved on 23 July 2009 from http://www.nypost.com/seven/03082008/ business/sharper_image_gift_cards_in_court_100970.htm.

6. "Lesson of the Valujet Disaster," *The New York Times*, August 21, 1997. Retrieved on 23 July 2009 from http://www.nytimes.com/1997/08/21/opinion/lessons-of-the-valujet-disaster.html.

7. See "Store Experience" and "Awards and Recognition," Target.com. Retrieved on 10 August 2010 from http://sites.target.com/site/en/company/page.jsp?contentId= WCMP04-032391.

8. Aniko Hill. "Launching a Successful Rebrand," *GCI Magazine*, November 5, 2008. Retrieved on 10 August 2010 from http://www.printthis.clickability.com/pt/cpt ?action=cpt&title=Launching+a+Successful+Rebrand+%7C+GCIMagazine.com &expire=&urlID=32242518&fb=Y&url=http%3A%2F%2Fwww.gcimagazine.c om%2Fbusiness%2Fmarketing%2F33908329.html&partnerID=357504&cid=3 3908329. Alan Lomax. "A Few Examples of Company Rebranding Done Right," *Articlesbase*, November 23, 2009. Retrieved on 10 August 2010 from http://www. articlesbase.com/public-relations-articles/a-few-examples-of-company-rebranding-done-right-1494663.html.

9. "Target Corporation Differentiation," *Wikipedia*. Retrieved 10 August 2010 from http://en.wikipedia.org/wiki/Target_Corporation#Differentiation. Jeffrey Arlen. "Why is Target so Cool? Target's Marketing Strategy," DSN Retailing Today, April 2, 2001. Retrieved on 10 August 2010 from http://findarticles.com/p/articles/ mi_m0FNP/is_7_40/ai_73181652/pg_2/?tag=content;col1.

10. Jason Hoppin. "Rebuilding Trust," *Pioneer Press*, July 27, 2008. Early metro cover story, and p.6A.

## Chapter 14: **Globalization and Trust**

1. Sirkka L. Jarvenpaa and Dorothy E. Leidner. *Communication and Trust in Global Virtual Teams*. Retrieved on 23 July 2009 from http://jcmc.indiana.edu/vol3/ issue4/jarvenpaa.html.

2. Defense Secretary Robert Gates. Quoted in "America's Best Leaders," *US News and World Report*, December1-8, 2008, p. 49.

3. *Edelman's 2009 Trust Barometer*. Edelman's research firm StrategyOne. Retrieved on 23 July 2009 from http://www.edelman.com/trust/2009.

4. *Press Release 219*, World Economic Forum. Retrieved on 22 July 2009 from http://www2.weforum.org/en/media/Latest%20Press%20Releases/PRESSRELEASES219.html.

5. Nick Burns, former U.S. under-secretary of state and professor at Harvard's Kennedy School of Government. *Edelman's 2009 Trust Barometer*. Edelman's research firm StrategyOne. Retrieved on 22 July 2009 from http://www.edelman.com/trust/2009.

6. "Cathie Black." *Corporate Biographies*. Hearst Corporation. Retrieved on 23 July 2009 from http://www.hearst.com/biography_corporate.php?name=Cathie+Black.

7. Erick S. Lipton and David Barboza. "As More Toys Are Recalled, Trail Ends in China," *New York Times*, June 19, 2007. Retrieved on 23 July 2009 from www.nytimes.com/2007/06/19/business/worldbusiness/19toys.html); David Kerley and Dan Childs. "Pet Food Makers to take Financial Responsibility for Pet Deaths from Poisoning," *ABC News*. March 23, 2007. Retrieved on 23 July 2009 from http://abcnews.go.com/US/story?id=297592&page=1.

8. Klaus Schwab, founder and executive chairman. *Annual Meeting of the New Champions*, World Economic Forum. Retrieved on 22 July 2009 from http://www.weforum.org/en/events/ArchivedEvents/AnnualMeetingoftheNewChampions2008/index.htm.

9. *Annual Meeting of the New Champions*, World Economic Forum. Retrieved on 22 July 2009 from http://www.weforum.org/en/events/ArchivedEvents/AnnualMeetingoftheNewChampions2008/index.htm.

10. Rob Taylor. "Canada Rated World's Sounded Bank System," *Reuters*, October 9, 2008. Retrieved on 23 July 2009 from http://www.reuters.com/article/ousiv/idUSTRE4981X220081009.

11. George Soros, Chairman, Soros Fund Management LLC. *Annual Meeting of the New Champions*, World Economic Forum. Retrieved on 22 July 2009 from http://www.weforum.org/en/events/ArchivedEvents/AnnualMeetingoftheNewChampions2008/index.htm.

12. H.H. Sheikh Mohammed Bin Rashid Al Maktoum, vice president and prime minister of the United Arab Emirates, Ruler of Dubai. *Summit on the Global Agenda*, World Economic Forum. Retrieved on 23 July 2009 from http://www.weforum.org/en/ events/ArchivedEvents/InauguralSummitontheGlobalAgenda/GACSummit08.

13. Jim Michaels. "In Afghanistan, strategy focuses on building trust," *USA Today*, March 30, 2009. Retrieved on 23 July from http://www.usatoday.com/printedition/news/20090330/1aafghan30x_cv.art.htm.

## Chapter 15: Trust in the Online Age

1.  John Chambers, chairman and CEO, Cisco USA. Quoted in "Technology Report Stresses Importance of ICT as a Catalyst for Growth in Global Turmoil," *Press Release, Cisco.* Retrieved on 23 July 2009 from http://newsroom.cisco.com/dlls/2009/prod_032609.html.

2.  "The importance of trust," *Council of Better Business Bureaus.* Retrieved on 23 July 2009 from http://vi.bbb.org/SitePage. aspx?id=d967bfa4-538a-4051-89af-d7938cf85520&site=158&art=7975.

3.  John Todor. *Customer Trust and Loyalty.* Pleasant Hill, CA: The Whetstone Edge, 2006.

4.  See "History," *Elance.com.* Retrieved on 23 July 2009 from http://www.elance.com/p/corporate/about/history.html.

5.  "T.J. Maxx data theft worse than first reported" (Associated Press). MSNBC, March 29, 2007. Retrieved on 23 July 2009 from http://www.msnbc.msn.com/id/17853440.

6.  Sharon Gaudin. "T.J. Maxx Security Breach Costs Soar To 10 Times Earlier Estimate," *InformationWeek,* August 15, 2007. Retrieved on 23 July 2009 from http://www.informationweek.com/news/globalcio/compliance/showArticle. jhtml?articleID=201800259.

7.  "Consumers Have False Sense of Security About Online Privacy—Actions Inconsistent With Attitudes," *RedOrbit,* December 6, 2006. Retrieved on 23 July 2009 from http://www.redorbit.com/news/technology/756988/ consumers_have_ false_sense_of_security_about_online_privacy_/index.html.

8.  "Habeas study finds significant lack of trust in e-mail," *BtoB: The Magazine for Marketing Strategies,* October 25, 2007. Retrieved on 23 July 2009 from http://www.btobonline.com/apps/pbcs.dll/article?AID=/20071025/ FREE/71025003/1115/FREE.

9.  Josh Bernoff. "People don't trust company blogs. What you should do about it," *Groundswel,* December 9, 2008. Retrieved on 23 July 2009 from http://blogs. forrester.com/groundswell/2008/12/people-dont-tru.html.

10. Brad Stone. "EBay Says Fraud Crackdown Has Worked," *The New York Times,* June 14, 2007. Retrieved on 23 July 2009 from http://www.nytimes.com/2007/06/14/ technology/14ebay.html?ex=1339473600&en=8fad5aada50a313b& ei=5088&partner=rssnyt&emc=rss.

11. Bob Sullivan, "Online fraud costs $2.6 billion this year," MSNBC, November 11, 2004. Retrieved on 18 February 2008 from http://www.msnbc.msn.com/id/6463545/.

## Chapter 16: A Sharp and Lasting Edge

1.  Author's personal meeting, emails, and phone interviews with Anthony Diekemper, CEO of Earth Security and COO of Skyline, April and May 2009.

# Index

Mentor, 111, 135-140, 143, 145-146, 178, 256

Merck, 90

Merriam-Webster dictionary, 135

Merrill Lynch, 150

Merrill, Rebecca, 17

Message, clarity of, 53-55

Michaels, Jim, 288

Micromanagement, 59

Microsoft Corporation, 62, 103, 126

Middle East, 90

Mighty Mississippi, The, 265-266

Milestone Systems, 102

Miller, Doug, iv

Milwaukee, Wisconsin, 152

Minehan, Maureen, 12

Minneapolis, 79-80, 159, 265

Minneapolis Grain Exchange, 79-80

Minnesota, 50-51, 104, 129, 159, 171, 182, 225, 265-267

Minnesota Department of Transportation, 265-267

Minnesota High School Football, 159

Minnesota, North Central, 104

Miscommunication, 297

Misleading, 156-157

Mission, 33, 40, 53, 56, 93, 113, 125, 206, 239, 282

Mission of the organization, 50, 66, 70, 157, 196

Mission statement, 57-58

Mission statement, personal, 58, 65, 114

Missouri, 192

Mistrust, 8, 182, 259, 264, 266, 268-269, 279

Molyneux, Stefan, 25-26

Moment, living in, 87-88, 112

Moment, Robert, 73

Moment, waking up to, 88

Moody, D.L., 13

Moral character, 100-101, 109

Moral code, 100

Moral compass, 100, 108

Morale, 2, 4, 6-8, 20, 30, 61, 68, 85, 103, 147, 163, 192, 206, 215, 241, 280

Morality, 99, 120

Morals, 100-101

Morton Thiokol (MT), 106

Mother Teresa, 89, 93-94, 149

Mothers, 75, 93-94, 156, 179

Motivation, 21-22, 59, 75, 239-240

Mozilo, Angelo, 150

MSNBC, 27, 76, 162, 296, 299

Multitasking, 210

Murtagh, Joe, 127

Namibia, 287

Narrow focus, 79-18

National Basketball Association (NBA), 161, 240

National Football League (NFL), 36-37, 159-162

Nature magazine, 257-258

Nazis, 260-261

NBC News, 161-162

Nebraska, 55

Negative experiences, 36-37, 40

Negative publicity, 271, 296

Neglect, 156, 215

Nelson, Marilyn Carlson, 16

Nepal, 29

Netherlands, The, 179, 278

Networking, 139, 177, 298

Networks, 35, 40

New ULM Telecon, 24

New Year's Resolutions, 249-250

New York, 21, 87, 191

New York City, 18-20, 158

New York Times, 257

Newton, Sir Isaac, 143

Nigeria, 297

Nitin, Nohria, 52, 76

Nobel Peace Prize, 93, 191, 256

Nobel Foundation, The, 94

Noble, Charles C., 230

Trusted, 2-4, 7-13, 18, 21-23, 26-30, 38, 55, 57, 60-61, 68, 73, 75, 78, 81-83, 89-94, 101-108, 114, 123-124, 132-135, 151, 175, 179-180, 187-191, 216, 219-222, 226-231, 240-247, 255-256, 260-266, 279-280, 284, 287, 296-300, 302-303, 310-313
Trusted brand, 60, 256, 279
Trusted diversity, 280-282
Trusted information sources, 298-299
Trusted leaders, 2-3, 150-151, 286-287
Trusted partners, 91-94
Trusted relationships, 95
Trusted, key traits of the, 45
Trusting, 33, 37, 119, 241-244, 250-252, 264, 268, 278, 282, 294-295
Trusting blogs, 134-135, 298
Trusting others, 4, 251
Trusting yourself, 249-250, 256
Trustonomics, 23-25
Trustworthiness, 11-12, 21, 259, 286
Trustworthiness, evaluating, 246
Tufts University, School of Medicine, 145
Tulsa, Oklahoma, 114
Twain, Mark, 135
Twitter, 35, 135
Tylenol, 127
U.S., 8, 27, 57, 67, 76, 152, 162, 191-192, 285-287
U.S. Automakers, 126-127
U.S. Economy, 191-192, 199
Uganda, 238
Under new management, 263-264
Understanding, 39, 78, 114, 180-181, 261, 280
Understanding, depth of, 173
Unification, 49-52, 58-60, 68, 114, 131, 221, 267, 282
Unilever, 173
United Arab Emirates (UAE), 287
United Kingdom (U.K.), 287, 295

United States (U.S.), 8, 21, 27, 33, 54-55, 57, 67, 76, 83, 110 , 123, 126, 129, 152, 162, 191-192, 199, 221, 277-278, 281-282, 285-287
Unity, 38, 64, 86
University of California study, 213
University of London study, 201
University of Michigan's American Consumer Satisfaction Index, 27
Unknown, the, 36-38, 237, 280
Upstartle, 125
US "Big Three" Automakers, 21, 126
US Airways, 123
US Army, 110, 152, 161-162
US Department of Labor
USA Today, 26, 37, 154, 288
Useem, Michael, 77
Vaill, Peter, 127
Valuable activities, 141
Value, 6-7, 21, 23-25, 37-38, 57, 82, 84, 91, 113-115, 118, 136, 141, 150, 156-159, 196, 215, 224, 237, 241-248, 257, 260, 301
Value, giving, 301
Valued, feeling, 74, 247
Values, 38, 109, 113-117, 121, 132, 140, 281-282
Values, family, 109
Values, personal, 113-115
ValuJet, 261-262
ValuJet Flight 592
VeriSign, 300
Virtue, 26, 62, 74, 219
Vision, 48-58, 62, 70, 77, 108, 137, 157, 170-171, 188-190, 206, 216, 227, 262
Vision, clarity of, 49, 51, 53, 55, 70, 206, 262, 267
Vision, impact of, 49-50
Vision, sharing your, 49, 68, 77, 227, 262
Visions, clouded, 50-52
Waddle, Scott Captain, 154-155